For My Country is far more than an account of the political events have that shaped the life of our nation. It is a lament for a sick nation whose potential has been truncated by corruption, malfeasance and greed.

In his well-timed memoir, Themba Maseko tells a moving story of his life as a black child, bred in the stifling confines of apartheid South Africa. The relegation of black people to the lowest rung of the human ladder soon made the young Maseko restless, and, like many others, he answered the call to join the struggle. We learn about the courage and righteousness that drove him and many of his comrades in pursuit of the dream of a free and democratic South Africa.

His journey was supposed to have a happy ending, but in the democratic era his convictions were tested. It was under the political party he considered his home, the party to which he gave his youth, the ANC, that Maseko was battered by the chilly winds of isolation and adversity.

Would he choose party over country? Or would he have the fortitude to take on the most powerful man in the country and his equally powerful and brazen enablers? And at what cost to himself and his family?

For My Country is a chilling reminder that those who stand to benefit from undemocratic and unlawful practices never sleep. The full extent of their attempts to capture the state are yet to be reckoned with. By sharing his story, Maseko takes us closer to that reckoning.

– *Redi Tlhabi*, broadcaster and author

THEMBA MASEKO

For My Country

*Why I Blew the Whistle on
Zuma and the Guptas*

Jonathan Ball Publishers
Johannesburg • Cape Town • London

First published in South Africa in 2021 by
JONATHAN BALL PUBLISHERS
A division of Media24 (Pty) Ltd
PO Box 33977
Jeppestown
2043

Reprinted once in 2021

ISBN 978-1-77619-053-9
ebook ISBN 978-1-77619-054-6

*Every effort has been made to trace the copyright holders and to obtain their permission
for the use of copyright material. The publishers apologise for any errors
or omissions and would be grateful to be notified of any corrections that
should be incorporated in future editions of this book.*

www.jonathanball.co.za
www.twitter.com/JonathanBallPub
www.facebook.com/JonathanBallPublishers

Cover by Sean Robertson
Design and typesetting by Nazli Jacobs
Printed and bound by CTP Printers, Cape Town
Set in Fairfield

I dedicate this book
to Phindile, my beautiful wife of 30 years,
to Thabo and Nqobi, my lovely sons,
to my late parents, Abbie Makhaza and
Ntombomvu Jane (Zwane) Maseko,
as well as to Bheki Mlangeni.

Contents

Foreword

THE YOUTHFUL THEMBA (or James) Maseko came into my universe during the tumultuous 1980s. These were the halcyon days when the word 'struggle' was deployed with a crescendo of enthusiasm. Themba belonged to a cohort of young people who embodied the Mass Democratic Movement's determination to transform institutions of higher learning into sites of progressive citizenship.

Themba and many other student activists rose to the responsibility of their time and mobilised thousands of youths and students across the country to be part of the organised student movement. As one of the leaders of the tertiary student movement, Themba became the link between the students and other sectors, such as civic associations, faith communities, women's organisations and trade unions. He also threw himself body and soul into the political underground struggles that were led by the African National Congress. I came to know him more closely because he was a friend and comrade of my younger brother, Vhonani.

I was very pleased when he called me during the COVID-19 lockdown to tell me that he was going to write a book that would tell his story in his own words. At first, I thought he was pulling my leg, but I soon believed him when he explained why he thought it was important for him to tell his story. It did not take long for me to realise that this fellow was serious about the book, and I encouraged him and offered my full support. During this conversation, he tried to convince me to write my own book, because, he argued, it was important for those who participated in the struggle to record their stories before this important part of the history of our country disappears into oblivion. I told him to lead by example and put pen to paper. I was pleasantly surprised to learn that he accepted the challenge.

I admire his determination to tell his story as candidly and as frankly as he has done. Although some of us knew about his experience in government and were extremely disappointed about the way he was treated after he rejected the illegal and unethical advances of the Guptas, few knew what happened behind the scenes of the events he describes in this book. I had the advantage of knowing the background to a lot of the things that ultimately led him to leave the public service. In fact, unless one was following his story right from the beginning, it would be difficult to understand what happened behind closed doors. This book will help to put everything into perspective.

I am particularly happy that the book doesn't just deal with the unenviable experience he had with the Gupta family, but also records his experiences and challenges as an activist before joining government. There is a detailed account of his role in the public sector, starting as an ANC MP, then becoming the first head of education in Gauteng and establishing the Gauteng Department of Education, serving as director-general of the departments of Public Works and Public Service and Administration and becoming head of GCIS and government spokesperson.

Themba represents a generation of activists-turned-civil-servants whose commitment to the Constitution and service to the people superseded everything else, including loyalty to the party. This was a generation of civil servants who put our people ahead of their personal interests and put people ahead of party. As a matter of fact, they understood that the best way to serve their party is to serve the country well with commitment and integrity. It is my hope that this book will encourage other activists and all those who were involved in the struggle against apartheid (and building a new constitutional state) to have the courage to tell their stories in their own words.

I hope that readers will enjoy this book.

SYDNEY MUFAMADI

The president calls

PRESIDENT JACOB ZUMA: 'Mfokababa, kunalamadoda akwa-Gupta. Ngifun' ukuthi uhlangane nabo futhi ubancede' (My brother, there are these Gupta men, I want you to meet with them and help them).

ME: 'Mr President, I have already agreed to meet Ajay Gupta. In fact, ngisendleleni yokuyohlangana no Ajay Gupta njengoba sikhuluma nje' (I'm on my way to the meeting with Ajay Gupta as we speak).

ZUMA: 'Hayi, kwa kuhle loko Mfokababa' (Very good, my brother).

ME: 'Yebo, Mr President' (Yes, Mr President).

ZUMA: 'Ingabe kukhon'okunye?' (Is there anything else?)

ME: 'Cha, President' (No, Mr President).

ZUMA: 'Kulungile ke, Mfokababa. Sizokhuluma' (It's okay, my brother, we will chat later).

One day in May 2010, I had just left my office at the Government Communication and Information System (GCIS) in the Midtown Building in Pretoria when I received a call from the landline at Mahlamba Ndlopfu, the official residence of the president of South Africa in Pretoria. I was not a little surprised.

Unlike former presidents Thabo Mbeki and Kgalema Motlanthe, with whom I had dealt directly in my capacity as government spokesperson and chief executive officer (CEO) of GCIS, there had not been any direct communication between me and President Jacob Zuma since he assumed office in May 2009. In fact, this would turn out to be the first and only call I ever received from him. My limited interaction with the president and his staff gave me the impression that I wasn't trusted, and I suspected my crime was that I had worked for the Mbeki administration. I was therefore guilty by association.

The call lasted a mere 90 seconds, if not less. After the initial exchange of pleasantries, Zuma inquired about my meeting with the Guptas, and the conversation concluded as soon as I confirmed that my meeting with Ajay Gupta was going ahead. I was so flabbergasted by the call that I forgot to ask the president what exactly he had in mind when he said I should help them.

Zuma's call came as I was on my way to Ajay Gupta's residence in Saxonwold, Johannesburg. Ajay, the eldest of the Gupta brothers, had been pestering me about a meeting for many weeks. I had first met Ajay at the board meeting of the International Marketing Council (IMC, since renamed Brand South Africa) in March of that year. As the CEO of GCIS I had automatic board membership, and Ajay had been a member since 2002.[1] However, he rarely attended board meetings and the March meeting was the first he had attended during my time on the board.

I was surprised when Ajay, in his capacity as IMC board member, suddenly took over the planning and logistics for Zuma's upcoming state visit to India in the first week of June 2010. While I did not join the state entourage for the trip to India, I later learnt from my IMC colleagues that the Guptas had basically usurped the powers of our departments of International Relations and Cooperation and Trade and Industry and become the nodal point for communication between the Indian government and Zuma during his stay.

However, the most shocking report I got about the state visit was that in his speech at a banquet for South African and Indian ministers and business leaders, Zuma had reportedly said that for businesses that were thinking of investing in South Africa, the suitable way of channelling their investment would be through the Gupta family.[2] By then, it was public knowledge that Zuma's son Duduzane was a business partner and director of a number of Gupta-owned companies.

Around June 2010 I finally agreed to meet with Ajay, mostly because I simply wanted to get him off my back.

On the drive to Johannesburg, where I also lived, my mind started racing as it dawned on me that this was likely to be no ordinary meeting. Did the president know that my meeting with Ajay was taking place that very afternoon? Was it possible that Ajay knew about the call, or, worse, that he perhaps asked or told Zuma to make the call? Did the president really just call to ask that I help out his friends?

During my time at GCIS I always had an open-door policy and met with different stakeholders in the media industry. However, all my meetings with editors, journalists, media owners and other media practitioners were voluntary and never on an instruction from a senior decision-maker in government.

Once I got to the Johannesburg Zoo in Saxonwold I opened my diary to confirm the address. I made a turn and drove a short distance until I saw the Sahara Computers board outside an upmarket residence.

A well-dressed security guard at the rather large black gates approached my car and politely asked if I was Mr Maseko from the government. I confirmed that I was. He asked me to drive in and directed me to stop in front of the large entrance area by the double front doors and told me to leave the keys in the car so that he could park it for me. I was still pondering whether I should leave my laptop and briefcase in the car, and let a stranger drive it away, when the security guard got in the driver's seat. As he drove off, I realised I was so stunned by the royal reception that I hadn't even taken a note-pad and pen.

At the front door another security guard presented me to a woman who seemed like a butler. She led me to a large formal lounge and told me that Ajay would be with me shortly.

As I was about to sit down, Ajay walked in, a broad smile on his face, and extended his hand. He was wearing a white shirt with no tie and his dark black hair looked like it had not been cut in a while. I couldn't help noticing a shiny gold watch on his left wrist. He was followed, a few seconds later, by his younger brother Atul, who quickly greeted me before walking over to Ajay and whispering something to him. Then he left.

Without wasting time on formalities, Ajay started telling me why he wanted to meet with me. He told me that his family was in the process of setting up a media company and he needed the government to support it in the form of advertising. Within two minutes, he got straight to the point.

'I am aware that government spends around R600 million on advertising across media platforms and I want that expenditure to be transferred to my company.'

I couldn't believe what I was hearing. In essence, he said that the total GCIS advertising budget must be spent on his soon-to-be established television station and newspaper. Although he also mentioned the television station, his main focus in the discussion was the newspaper, *The New Age*, which was scheduled to launch that year.

I sat in stunned silence as he went on to explain that he knew the African National Congress (ANC) had been talking about setting up its own newspaper because of concerns that the South African media was not covering the good news about the work the government was doing, but that they had failed to do so up to that point. He therefore wanted to exploit this opportunity and start a newspaper that would do exactly that.

My mind was racing as I tried to collect my thoughts and figure out how he knew that the GCIS was spending R600 million on media buying, since this amount was not indicated as a line item in our budget. As an *ex officio* member of the ANC's subcommittee on communication, I was aware of the exploratory internal discussions about setting up an ANC newspaper to counteract the negative reporting on government in the media. However, I was not entirely convinced of the wisdom of setting up a party newspaper; I felt that government's work should speak for itself through its actions and should make use of GCIS platforms such as the government website and the *Vuk'ukuzenzele* newsletter.

After hearing Ajay out, I explained how the system of media buying works in government. I told him that the advertising budget in fact did not sit in the GCIS budget. National departments develop their own marketing and communications strategies and produce their own budgets for these activities. They then submit their departmental budgets to National Treasury, which includes their marketing and communication budgets as a line item. Treasury allocates the funds to the line departments, and the departments then approach GCIS to assist them with implementing their plans, which includes procuring media space from media houses.

The system was designed to give government the muscle to negotiate better prices using the strength of having a massive budget spend, as GCIS would approach media houses as a single government buyer. I made it clear to Ajay that I did not control the advertising budgets of other departments and that if he wanted to lay his hands on the money, he would have to speak to each of the national departments individually. The GCIS budget only covered our administrative costs, such as salaries, rentals and our work of communicating government programmes.

The further I got into my explanation, the more I got the sense that I was talking to myself. As I outlined how the system worked, I could see that Ajay was becoming increasingly agitated and irritated. The next moment he leant forward, looked me straight in the eye and frowned.

'Listen, this is how this thing is going to work. You must go to all the departments, talk to the ministers, tell them to transfer their budgets into your account (GCIS), and your only job is to make sure the money comes to me and *The New Age* newspaper, you hear me?' he barked.

'I'm sorry, Ajay, that is not how things work.'

'Talk to the ministers!' he said.

He also told me that if I had difficulties with any of the ministers, I should let him know and he would call them to order. He would make sure that they delivered.

Now I was getting annoyed. Not only was Ajay telling me how to do my job, but he was implying that he could influence the actions and decisions of Cabinet ministers. I was so upset by his impertinence that my tongue stumbled on the English words: 'Ajay, but these are my leaders, these are my ministers, you can't talk to . . . I mean, talk *about* them like that.'

He was unperturbed. 'No, this is how the system works now. If there is any minister who is not cooperative, you should tell me and I'll sort them out,' he insisted.

Ajay became rather aggressive at that point, and I did not appreciate his tone.

'What do you mean when you say you will sort them out?' I asked.

Then he told me in so many words that he held regular meetings with Zuma at his house, and that any ministers who refused to cooperate with me would be summoned to Saxonwold – presumably to be instructed to transfer their budgets to GCIS. I understood him to mean that my role was to ensure that GCIS became nothing more than a conduit through which public funds could be channelled into his company.

What incredible arrogance, I thought.

He proceeded to tell me that Zuma was a regular visitor to the Saxon-wold residence and came for dinner at least once a week. I suspected that this comment was intended to show his close ties to the president. I realised there was no further point in trying to convince him that what he was asking of me was impossible. I was not going to cooperate with him; I was not prepared to break the rules.

I was extremely angry and confused and couldn't wait to get out of the house. We parted ways without any pleasantries and didn't even shake hands.

When I got outside, my car was already parked by the door. As I drove off, I realised that I might just have put my job on the line. Inadvertently, I had defied the president. The big question in my mind was what Zuma had meant during his call when he told me to help the Gupta brothers. Did he know that Ajay wanted me to transfer the government's entire advertising budget to his company?

As time went by, Zuma never inquired how my meeting with the Gupta brothers had gone. I was uncertain about approaching him as I didn't know how he would react. As a result, Cabinet meetings became increasingly awkward for me, but I carried on in the belief that in the end everything would be fine.

2

A boy called Trust

MY PARENTS WERE born on the same farm in a remote part in what is today Mpumalanga province. Their families were forcibly removed from their land in the late 1800s and they were initially dumped in a place called Emlomo and later again removed to Wesselton township outside Ermelo.

My mother, Ntombomvu Zwane, never saw the inside of a classroom since girls were not encouraged to go to school. In isiZulu her name means 'the red girl', because she was light-skinned and had red hair. My father, Abbie Makhaza Maseko, went to school until Standard 4 (Grade 6), after which he had to get a job on the farms to help support his family. My parents got married in their late teens, and my father, like many young African men of his generation, decided to go to Johannesburg in search of better job opportunities.

At the start he had to hustle, like so many others, and he worked at different factories on the East Rand, taking care to avoid the police as he did not always have a valid pass to be in the city. The pass was a special permit that white employers gave to Africans allowing them to be in urban areas. In his early twenties he got a big break when he got his driver's licence, which allowed him to get stable work as a driver for different companies. Soon he was in a position to move into a

My parents, Abbie and Ntombomvu Maseko, on their wedding day.

four-roomed house in Dube, Soweto, where he was eventually joined by my mother and they started a family.

I was born in Dube on 27 January 1964, the sixth of seven kids. In isiZulu my name, Themba, means 'hope' or 'trust'. At that point my mother had birthed five boys and my parents were desperate for a daughter. They called their fifth child Banele, which means 'that is enough' (boys). When I was born, they decided to call me Themba in the hope that next time it would be a girl. Their wish finally came true when my sister, Duduzile, was born.

My parents couldn't have known it at the time, but I would live up to the meaning of my name. Not only do I have a positive, hopeful out-look on life but I also pride myself on being a principled and trusting person who believes in the goodness of people. I always try to do the right thing.

Although we were a family of nine, I cannot recall a time when our house was only occupied by the nine of us. There were always relatives from other parts of the country who used our home as a base when they came to Johannesburg in search of employment opportunities. These were nephews, nieces, uncles or just random people from the rural areas who knew my parents or grandparents. When I was growing up, I never knew what it meant to sleep in a bed; sleeping on a mat on the concrete floor was second nature to me. However, I don't recall ever spending a night without a meal despite the fact that my father was the only one with an income.

Nothing mattered more to my parents than giving their children the best possible education, even if the apartheid government was hell-bent on making sure that Africans and other so-called non-whites did not have access to quality education. My father worked a 14-hour shift and managed to save enough money so that we could pay school fees, buy books and have wearable school uniforms.

Sadly, none of my siblings finished school, but it was not completely their fault. Going to school in the townships in the 1960s and 1970s was tough, as it involved long walks to school, spending the whole day on an empty stomach and surviving corporal punishment. Winters were often unbearable; I remember our piercingly cold classrooms often lacked window panes as the schools had no budget for maintenance. My parents were bitterly disappointed that most of my siblings left school by Standard 7 (Grade 9).

Since my father worked long hours and was away from home often, the full responsibility for getting us to school and making sure we did our homework fell on my mother. I owe my dedication to learning to her, for all her emotional and physical support, even if she couldn't provide any learning support. To her the key to a better life was education, and she was driven by a motherly dedication to ensure we got one.

Of course, it wasn't always easy to keep us in line, and her only weapon was the threat of reporting us to our father, who was a disciplinarian of note and often resorted to corporal punishment whenever he learnt that one of his kids had missed school or failed a grade. I still have memories of my father arriving in the early hours of the morning and waking up one or two of my brothers to punish them with a belt for missing school or not doing their homework. He didn't bother to wait for the morning to mete out his punishment.

I can't recall if I was ever a victim of this early-morning punishment, but I certainly remember the fear that his footsteps brought whenever he opened the door to our bedroom or our sleeping quarters. There was no electricity in the townships at the time, so he would enter the room with either a lit candle or a paraffin lamp and we all had to show our faces so that he could find his 'victim'.

I completed the first years of primary school without incident, even though it was a long walk to school. One of the things I and many of my peers had to deal with was hunger at school. On better days there was bread and, if we were lucky, the thinnest smear of jam or peanut butter for breakfast. On bad days my mom gave us tea or soft porridge. On very bad days all we got was water. How we survived a whole day at school and learnt something on an empty stomach remains a mystery to me. I always thought school was such a crazy place because we had this thing called a lunch break but few of the kids had anything to eat, except a few whose parents were better off.

For Standards 3 to 6 (Grades 5 to 8) I was sent to Belle Higher Primary School, which was a good 5-kilometre walk from our house, and was run by the unpopular and incompetent Department of Education and Training (DET), which was responsible for the *under*-education of African children.

One day in 1975, when I was 11 years old, our principal announced at the daily school assembly that the new medium of instruction for all African learners would be changed from English to Afrikaans. Most of us had only started learning Afrikaans in Standard 2 (Grade 4) and I for one was barely getting to grips with the basics of the language at the time.

At the beginning of 1976, the apartheid government went ahead with its plan to introduce Afrikaans as a medium of instruction for all our subjects. As a rule, our classrooms were not designed to let in much sunlight, but they became even darker when this new policy was implemented. In an effort to force this policy down our throats, the apartheid state supplied textbooks that were already translated into Afrikaans. We joked that if the state had its way, they would have taught us our African languages in Afrikaans too.

My very first lesson of my Standard 6 (Grade 8) year was mathematics. A new teacher, Mr Mfeka from Natal (today KwaZulu-Natal), had just been appointed at the school. He walked into class with a textbook, a newspaper under his arm and a short wooden cane that he used for disciplining us. As he walked in he shouted, 'Wiskunde!'

The whole class fell completely silent.

'Wiskunde' is Afrikaans for mathematics. So here we had a new teacher who was supposed to teach us a subject that was not always our favourite and in a language that was foreign to all of us. He went on to write something on the board. We recognised the numbers but could not understand a word he was saying. Some of the older students, who were about the same age as the teacher, tolerated the circus that was unfolding in front of our eyes for a few minutes but then raised their hands to inform the teacher that the class was not following his lesson.

He would have none of it. He was there to teach, and nothing was going to stand in his way. He went on to warn us – in isiZulu – that he had been told Johannesburg kids were unruly, and he was not going to tolerate ill discipline in his class. As the students continued to try and reason with him, he banged on the table and made it clear that he had not come all the way from Natal to debate with students. Fortunately, the bell rang before the situation could get out of hand.

It turned out that all the classes were having similar experiences with new teachers who had been brought to our school to teach the different subjects in Afrikaans. Not only were the students feeling aggrieved but our regular teachers were also upset. They had never been trained to teach their specialist subjects in Afrikaans and now they were being replaced by teachers from elsewhere. I still don't know where the DET found all the African teachers who could teach in Afrikaans, because teacher training colleges were also segregated along racial lines and most of their training was in an African language.

Going to school became a real nightmare. I sat in class the whole day without understanding a thing. Imagine an English- or Afrikaans-speaking kid sitting in class for a mathematics or physics lesson and being told that those subjects would now be taught in isiZulu or isi-Xhosa. That's what happened. Sadly, this episode led to a lot of absenteeism in my school, but I did not want to let my parents down and decided to keep attending classes.

Within a few weeks the Afrikaans-medium debacle spilled over into the public arena, with more and more black parents and students raising their objections. One day, while walking home after school, I noticed a group of older students at the Phefeni railway station having what appeared to be a serious conversation, but I didn't stop to listen to what they were talking about. Later I discovered that they had gathered to discuss the near collapse of education at our school.

Apart from the fact that Afrikaans was generally not the most popular subject, what added to the negative attitude towards it was that the apartheid state had made it compulsory. For instance, you could be enrolled for seven subjects, including mathematics, biology, physics, accounting and history, but Afrikaans, English *and* your home language also had to be part of your subject choice. This meant that African students were compelled to enrol for a third language.

By the end of February, the mood in the school changed as the students became increasingly restless. The older students started holding meetings after school hours and during breaks. These meetings involved the whole student body and occasionally interfered with classes.

The student meetings got louder and more militant, something that scared me a little. It was my first exposure to protest politics. At one of the student meetings at the end of February, the students decided to demand the end to Afrikaans as the medium of instruction with immediate effect, failing which we threatened to boycott classes.

A delegation was sent to the principal's office to hand over our demands. We gave the principal a few days to respond, knowing very well that he had no authority to accept our demands. The deadline came and went.

In March 1976 our school went on a class boycott, which involved refusing to attend classes and demonstrating outside the school premises with handwritten placards. Little did I know that many other schools were embarking on the same programme of protest. Our student leaders did not tell us that they were asking students from other schools to join the protest. By the end of March more schools had joined the class boycott, and I subsequently learnt that this movement was gaining momentum and spreading to other parts of the country.

I never got a chance to hear or understand what my parents thought about these developments, as they were not politically inclined. Other township parents started organising themselves and formed parents' committees. The South African Students' Organisation (SASO), which was aligned with the Black Consciousness Movement, coordinated a variety of student meetings and joint meetings with parents. By May, the number of schools that were involved in the class boycotts had increased drastically, but at most schools it was still business as usual.

At this stage the intransigence of the apartheid state became evident, and the student leaders felt that it was time to get students into the streets. A few individuals, such as Seth Mazibuko and Tsietsi Mashinini, were emerging as the leaders of the movement. The suggestion of a march across Soweto gained wide support. The agreed date was 16 June 1976. By then, Belle Higher Primary School had already been on a class boycott for about three months.

On 16 June everything began according to plan. We were meant to converge at Morris Isaacson High School in Jabavu and march all the way to Orlando West High School in Vilakazi Street, where we would be met by students from other parts of the township (Belle Higher Primary is about 500 metres from Orlando West High School). Thousands of students gathered outside their various schools and started marching towards their nodes (prearranged meeting points).

That morning happened to be one of the coldest and driest of that winter. I woke up as usual, dressed in my full uniform and pretended to my mother that I was off to attend school. I felt an inexplicable burst of energy but also some trepidation at the thought of participating in my first protest march. I was worried what my parents would say if they found out that I was going to be part of the march, and also petrified that I could be arrested and spend a night in jail. Still, my anger at the apartheid government for interrupting my school career by introducing such an unjust and unfair policy outweighed my fears.

That day I became an activist.

We gathered outside my school around 8 am and started singing struggle songs such as 'Senzeni na' (What have we done?). By 10 am a few police vans started gathering nearby and I was amazed to see the cops looking pretty terrified. We started proceeding towards the rendezvous at the church outside Orlando West High School. (Recently, one of my brothers told me that Orlando West High School was selected was because it was one of the schools that had decided not to participate in the protest march. Apparently the principal at the time was very strict and did not allow any political meetings at the school.)

At about 11 am, we received news that thousands of students were marching from Musi High School and that some had already been involved in skirmishes with the police. In the process a few delivery vans and police cars had reportedly been pelted with stones, but the march had been largely peaceful. Once big groups of students began to arrive at the gates of Orlando West High School, the police also converged on the area. I had never seen so many cops in my life. The police shouted instructions that we should disperse, and the situation became very tense.

As the number of students increased, the police became increasingly restless. The next moment I heard gunshots and then loud screams from all over. Some of the shots turned out to be teargas fired by the police. I had never experienced teargas before. Seconds after I saw the white smoke my eyes started burning and I couldn't breathe. I remember falling and being afraid that I would be trampled as everyone ran for cover. The next thing I heard was the blaring sound of ambulance and police sirens. I had never been so scared in my life.

Word quickly spread that a number of students had been shot by the police. I ran into the Methodist church building nearby where I took cover for what felt like an eternity.

'Bang, bang, bang.' More shots. Screaming.

The churchyard was overflowing as more students ran from the barrage of gunshots and teargas canisters flew in all directions. Many of the students had head injuries and others had to be carried as they had been wounded in the legs. The church was turning into a hospital of sorts. I will never forget the many white school shirts covered in blood. The combination of the smell of teargas and blood soon made it unbearable inside the church.

I went outside to get some fresh air and saw scores of wounded students lying on the ground. One lay face down with blood gushing from an open wound in the back of his head. I couldn't tell whether he was dead or alive. I froze as I saw a police van stop outside the church and white policemen jump out, their machine guns at the ready.

A strong hand grabbed my arm from behind and dragged me back into the church building. The student, who was much older than me, reprimanded me and instructed me to go to the back of the church to hide from the police. I sprinted inside and hid behind the pulpit while praying for my life.

At that point, I realised that my jersey was torn and my shirt and trousers were caked with blood. I touched every part of my body to check if I was hurt or shot and was relieved to find that the blood wasn't mine. I must have spent about two hours under the pulpit.

After a few hours the situation calmed down a little, although there continued to be sporadic incidents of shooting. The priest advised those who wanted to leave to sneak out through the back entrance of the church. As I made my way there, I walked past dozens of injured students who were screaming in pain. I was absolutely terrified.

I saw several students lying outside the church building and in the street in positions that suggested they were dead. I will never forget the image of a girl with a huge wound in her neck, her mouth and eyes wide open and her arms spread out on the ground. I stared at her for a long time before I stumbled away from her lifeless body.

I tripped and fell over a rock. When I got up, I saw many more bodies lying in Vilakazi Street and wondered how many of them were still alive. I was dead scared, and although I wasn't crying, tears were rolling down my face. I had been to family funerals but I had never seen a dead body that close.

Confused, I ran towards our home, which was about four kilometres away, thinking I might not make it there alive as the shooting continued. I decided to use back roads to avoid any contact with the police, who appeared to be on a shooting spree. Then anger got the better of me and I decided to join a group of students who were hurling stones at the heavily armed police. A white policeman was later brutally killed by the students and the community after he found himself isolated from his trigger-happy colleagues.

To this day I can't recall how I made it back home, but I finally did after many run-ins with the police, ducking live rounds and rubber bullets and inhaling volumes of teargas. The worst moment was seeing a fellow student shot right in front of my eyes and running away to save my own life. I was 12 years old.

There was a look of both fear and relief on my mother's face when I walked into the house around 6 pm. She had heard about the march and the killing of so many students near my school. Since our house was only about a kilometre from the main road, where most of the fighting and shooting was taking place, she could hear the gunshots and the sirens very clearly.

My mother gave me one of the few yet most memorable hugs I ever received from her. It gave me strength and hope. Of course, she was also angry with me for participating in the march. Tears flowed from her eyes and from mine. I had not eaten for most of the day and she gave me porridge and sour milk, which at that moment was the best meal in the world, served by a loving mother.

She asked whether I had seen any of my siblings. I had not. Were they still alive?

This question was only answered much later that evening when my brothers walked into the house one by one. They faced a much stronger rebuke from my mother for coming home that late and for not looking after me.

My father had heard about the uprising on the radio but there was no way of calling him because he was on the road, and of course there were no mobile phones in those days. I never saw my old man look as stressed as he did when he arrived home that fateful evening. He seemed older than his years.

By then we had also heard the news that 13-year-old Hector Pieterson had been shot dead by the police. The policeman who shot him remains unknown to this day. I knew it could have been me in the line of fire, or any of my brothers or classmates. (My sister was much younger at the time and was not involved.)

A few days later, Meshack, a cousin who was staying with us at the time, went missing. I learnt from my friends that he had apparently been shot, and I rushed home to inform my mother. A few of us set out to look for him, but without success. As we got back, we saw a neighbour's car parked outside our house and knew something was up. I ran into the house and found an injured Meshack there; he had been found lying by the side of the road a few streets away. Although he was in excruciating pain, his injury was fortunately not that serious. During the protests he had been hit in the right leg with a rubber bullet instead of a real one. We took him to a nearby clinic where he got a few stitches and returned home that evening.

The apartheid government tried to hide the actual number of students who lost their lives during the student uprisings in Soweto but it is estimated that between 100 and 1 000 people died on that day.

On 16 June 1976 I lost my youth for ever. This was the day I realised that I had a choice to either live like a slave or die like a fighter for my people and my country. That day defined who I was to become. It solidified my commitment to become part of the fight against colonialism and white domination. It also hooked me on politics.

The uprising would continue for the next few years, and for most of that year no further classes took place. More and more student gatherings were held in different parts of Soweto and in other parts of the country. These meetings were often followed by protest marches that often led to clashes with the police and more deaths.

I attended quite a number of those meetings and participated in numerous protest marches. I was lucky that I was never injured. My mother got wind of my participation and she was not impressed, but she never told on me to my father.

The township came to look more and more like a war zone. The apartheid government deployed the army in Soweto, and the soldiers were notorious for using live ammunition to disperse student gatherings. Against the strict instructions of my parents, I continued to take part in protest meetings and demonstrations, which often ended up in skirmishes with the police. The state responded to our protests with brutal force, so we resolved that we would meet force with force and violence with violence. In reaction, government buildings, municipal buses, delivery trucks and any branded vehicles were set on fire.

There were many days when I returned home with bloodstains on my white school shirt and smelling of teargas fumes. On others I walked past injured protesters with open wounds who were screaming for help. Private vehicles became makeshift ambulances that took the wounded to the nearest clinics or hospitals. Medical practitioners such as Dr Nthato Motlana turned their private rooms into makeshift casualty wards and did their best to attend to the wounded youths.

Although I came out of 1976 physically unscathed, I was emotionally broken. I hated the evenings because I had endless nightmares, and often my mother would wake me up in the middle of the night, giving me a hug to try and soothe me. I harboured a lot of anger against the white government and I was ready to make the ultimate sacrifice to ensure that my country was liberated from all forms of oppression. I remained determined to be part of what I saw as a just war against the inhumane apartheid system.

Although I sometimes feared for my life, I didn't regret being part of the generation of young fighters who were prepared to give their lives for freedom. Like a soldier, I woke up every morning, put on my school uniform and went to protest meetings and participated in marches instead of attending classes. My white shirt, black shoes and grey trousers became my military regalia; my books became a shield against bullets; pens and little rocks became my weapons against the heavily armed policemen and soldiers on the township streets. The South African Defence Force might have been the strongest military power on the continent at that time, but somehow I – and thousands of other students – found the courage and the spirit to stand up to them.

While my mother came to accept that I was part of the struggle, I had to hide my strong convictions and activism from my father. He thought I was too young to be involved in politics and thought it was

Relaxing at my parents' house in Dube in 1977.

his duty as a father to keep me alive. I knew that my mother supported me because she started giving me some small change every morning, even though she didn't have enough for herself. I would use the money for taxi fare to go to meetings or to buy food for me and my comrades.

The unrest in the townships continued into the early 1980s. It was a challenging time to live through. Many families lost their loved ones and thousands of young people lost their chance at an education. The dreams and aspirations of thousands of young men and women were destroyed, as many of the students never went back to school. Others left the country illegally to join the ANC and the Pan Africanist Congress in exile and get military training in preparation for a full armed struggle against the apartheid system.

Many left the country without even telling their families. When someone disappeared, you didn't always know whether that person had gone into exile or had been abducted and killed by the security forces. At one of the student gatherings at Daliwonga Secondary School in Dube, we were encouraged to go into exile, but I wasn't considered because I was too young. I longed for the day when I would get my chance to go into exile for military training. At the many political meetings I attended I learnt about the sacrifices made by leaders such as Nelson Mandela, Walter Sisulu, Andrew Mlangeni, Robert Sobukwe, Govan Mbeki and others. I also learnt about leaders such as Oliver Tambo, Joe Slovo and Chris Hani and about the thousands of South Africans who had gone into exile. They were my heroes.

In 1979 I entered Orlando West High School, but sadly I failed Standard 7 (Grade 9). It was the first time I had failed a standard, but it was the result of spending more time on being an activist than on my studies. I didn't know how to break the news to my parents and found myself sobbing outside the kitchen door at Ous (Sotho slang for 'sister') Caroline Mdluli's house, a neighbour and my mother's friend.

I told her about my results and she invited me to join the family for dinner that evening. This was the first time in my life that I had sat round a table for a meal. She extended an open invitation to me to join the Mdluli family for dinner every evening. She then told my mother that she was going to find me a better school, on condition that I repeat and pass Standard 7. So I went back to school and passed with flying colours the following year. Ous Caroline liked me very much and took me under her wing, treating me as one of her own children. My parents welcomed her role.

She could see that I was really committed to my studies, but she was rightly worried that my political involvement was diverting my attention from my schoolwork. She promised that if I got good results in standards 7 and 8 (grades 9 and 10), she would get me enrolled at one of the best schools in the township. I went into the 1980 school year fully motivated, and I performed exceptionally well, becoming one of the top two students in my class.

Ous Caroline delivered on her promise when she saw my results and used her influence in her church to get me into Immaculata High School, a Catholic private school in Zone 6, Diepkloof, even though I didn't meet the basic admission criterion that learners at the school should belong to the Catholic Church. The school was run by nuns from Germany and Ireland. I had never before seen such dedicated and strict people, and of course I had to work extra hard to make up for the years I had been out of school.

Once I got to Standard 10 (Grade 12), a group of friends and I managed to convince the nuns to let us use one of the classrooms to study overnight. Most of us came from homes that were a little overcrowded and not conducive to proper studying. So we would bring our blankets, study the whole night and go back home in the morning – except on weekends, which we would spend at school. These were the best times of my school career.

When I passed matric, my parents, especially my father, were elated. I was the first person in my family to matriculate. While my father was still digesting the news, I told him that I wanted to go to university and that my dream was to become a lawyer. For a few minutes he didn't utter a single word and only stared at me. But then he nodded and said something about it being a good idea.

In a subsequent conversation with my mother, I learnt that my father had told her he was going to get a loan from either his employer or a bank. He was also prepared to sell his car to help me realise my dream. I was overwhelmed. There couldn't have been a stronger sign of my parents' love and trust.

Our results were released before Christmas and it was an especially joyous festive season. Ous Caroline even bought me a pair of shoes, trousers and a nice shirt.

Immaculata High School tried to give us some career guidance but

I had not applied to any university because I wasn't confident that I would get a university exemption and, if so, whether my parents would be able to pay my tuition fees. However, after receiving my results, everything changed. I realised that a door had swung open for me and it would be foolish not to do everything in my power to study and help break the cycle of poverty in my family.

3

Joining the SACP and ANC underground

THE VERY FIRST thing I did in January 1983 was to go to the University of the Witwatersrand (Wits) to apply in person. When I got there, I was told that although I met the requirements to study law, and the university had space for me, I couldn't be admitted 'because you are black' – the exact words of the lady at the admissions office.

'What do you mean?' I asked angrily.

'The only way you can be admitted is if you get permission from the minister of education to study at a white university.'

I was dumbstruck.

I asked for the details of the minister I had to apply to, and the lady even helped me to draft the letter. She seemed to have taken pity on me. When the reply came, shortly afterwards, I was informed that my request had been declined. The minister of education at the time was none other than FW de Klerk, later leader of the last National Party government, who rejected my application on the basis that Wits was a white university. In the letter, De Klerk advised that I should go to the University of Zululand since I was Zulu-speaking. I tore up the letter in disgust.

I was shattered but not broken. I would not give up that easily and applied to the University of Zululand and was admitted to the law faculty. Due to political unrest on the campus and a few personal considerations, I would only spend a year there, though. Violence broke out between students and supporters of Inkatha (later the Inkatha Freedom Party) and students affiliated to the ANC-aligned Azanian Students' Organisation (Azaso), who did not want the Inkatha leader and university chancellor, Mangosuthu Gatsha Buthelezi, to speak at the graduation ceremony that year. On 29 October 1983, four students and an Inkatha member were killed and the university was shut down. We only wrote our exams in January the following year.

After I heard that I had passed my exams, I reapplied to Wits University. Fortunately, I no longer needed ministerial consent as the regime had relaxed entry requirements for black students at white universities. However, I could only be accommodated in the arts faculty as law was already full.

My political activism grew by leaps and bounds after I enrolled at Wits, and for the first time I formally joined a student organisation, becoming a member of Azaso. I quickly rose through the ranks as I was a hard worker who always volunteered for tasks and never missed meetings. I was elected to a number of positions, such as chairperson of the Glen Thomas House Committee (a residence for black Wits students next to Baragwanath Hospital in Soweto). I was twice president of the Black Students' Society and served in the regional and national structures of Azaso (later renamed the South African National Students' Congress, or Sansco), first as assistant general secretary and later as general secretary.

These roles made it possible for me to interact with activists and leaders beyond student politics and outside of campus. I also became a cadre of the Mass Democratic Movement (MDM), which worked with civic organisations, unions, churches, women's groups and other bodies. More importantly, being part of the MDM gave me an opportunity to interact with other race groups. Growing up in Soweto, I had

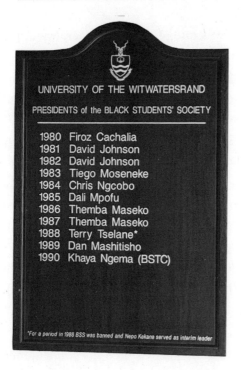

UNIVERSITY OF THE WITWATERSRAND

PRESIDENTS of the BLACK STUDENTS' SOCIETY

1980	Firoz Cachalia
1981	David Johnson
1982	David Johnson
1983	Tiego Moseneke
1984	Chris Ngcobo
1985	Dali Mpofu
1986	Themba Maseko
1987	Themba Maseko
1988	Terry Tselane*
1989	Dan Mashitisho
1990	Khaya Ngema (BSTC)

*For a period in 1988 BSS was banned and Nepo Kekana served as interim leader

A plaque in the Wits SRC boardroom listing the names of past presidents of the Black Students' Society.

never met or known a white, coloured or Indian person on a personal level, except for the nuns at Immaculata.

My activism at Wits opened many other doors for me and I got noticed by the struggle leadership. The highlight was when I was recruited to join the underground structure of the banned South African Communist Party (SACP) and later also the ANC.

My political mentor in the SACP was Sydney Mufamadi, who went on to become minister of safety and security after the first democratic elections in 1994. Sydney, or Bra Syd as I got to call him, was the assistant general secretary of the General Allied Workers' Union (GAWU), one of the most progressive trade unions in the country, and was a stalwart of the United Democratic Front (UDF), the coalition of more than 400 anti-apartheid organisations that came together in 1983 to oppose the government's proposed tricameral parliament. As a young student leader I was inspired by Bra Syd's wisdom, kindness and knowledge of our struggle. He was one of the most disciplined, principled leaders of our movement and incredibly humble.

Becoming a member of the SACP was a milestone, since membership of the party was a privilege that was reserved for a select few. You couldn't simply join the party; you had to be invited, on the basis of your commitment, dedication, understanding of politics and the ability to operate underground. This not only boosted my confidence but also exposed me to a new breed of activists and leaders. Most importantly, it taught me the importance of reading up on political concepts and understanding politics, and also about what it meant to work in the underground structures of a banned organisation. For example, when we had to complete a syllabus on Marxism-Leninism, I would be given either a book or an article to read over a two-week period and be expected to come back and discuss the article or book to show what I had learnt from the material.

The meetings between a young activist and his political mentor had to take place clandestinely. So you would get a note to meet a person at a particular place on a set date and at a set time. Arriving late was not tolerated and missing an appointment could mean that you were out of the loop for over a month. You would also have to account for your misconduct to the person who had recruited you. I wouldn't have dreamt of letting Sydney down. My experiences during this time taught me about discipline, punctuality, having respect for leaders and understanding difficult political concepts, and gave me the ability to participate in complex discussions. It also gave me a love of books.

I also represented the student voice at meetings of the UDF and served on the executive committee of the National Education Crisis Committee (NECC), which was established in 1986 by black parents concerned about the state of black education. It tried to mediate the conflict between the black community and the apartheid state as represented by the DET.

The NECC spent a lot of energy convincing students that while the struggle against Bantu Education was important, education could not collapse completely and students had to go back to school. High school students were organised under the Congress of South African Students (Cosas), which had emerged following the banning of SASO. Cosas leaders generally listened to the NECC, and so the NECC inadvertently became the alternative Department of Education for black students.

My involvement with the UDF and NECC in the mid-1980s brought me into contact with key leaders of the struggle, both inside and outside the country, as I also joined various delegations to meet the ANC leadership in exile.

One of these leaders was the Reverend Frank Chikane, who would later play a role in my life as a civil servant and be an important mentor. Chikane was a leader of the UDF and the South African Council of Churches. Like Archbishop Desmond Tutu, Reverend Molefe Tsele, Reverend Beyers Naudé and many others, Chikane used the pulpit to preach the message of freedom and challenged the theology of the white churches who used the Bible to justify apartheid policies. These members of the clergy played a key role in closing the gap that was created by the absence of political leaders who were either in detention, prison or exile.

I became one of the key contact people between Azaso/Sansco and the ANC Youth Section in Lusaka, Zambia. The ANC Youth Section not only gave us political guidance but also offered resources and political material for distribution to tertiary institutions inside the country. I went on numerous trips to Botswana, Zimbabwe and Zambia, and sometimes to London and other European cities, to meet senior leaders of the ANC.

A major highlight of my many trips to the United Kingdom in the 1980s was getting to meet Oliver Reginald Tambo, fondly known as OR, the exiled leader of the ANC. I went to the ANC offices in London for a meeting and I was told that OR had just been released from hospital after a stroke. I asked whether I could pay him a visit at his house and was surprised to be told that his wife, Adelaide, had agreed to it. OR was still recovering, and he was not able to speak, but he welcomed me with a hug that I will never forget.

The visits to African countries were clandestine trips that involved jumping fences, sleeping in the bush and using fake documents, because the regime made it very difficult for black South Africans to get passports. The trips to Botswana were a little easier, though, because the ANC people had good contacts on both sides of the border.

Most of my trips were via Gaborone, using either a temporary Zambian or Botswana passport, which would be delivered to me at Glen Thomas House or I would collect them from someone standing on a street corner in Hillbrow or Berea. Most of the passports I got in South Africa were from one of the homelands, such as the Ciskei or Transkei, as these so-called independent states were allowed to issue passports to blacks. These allowed me to get across the border into neighbouring countries, where I would be issued with a new passport that would enable me to travel abroad. I had a few passports from the Republic of the Transkei, especially after Brigadier Bantu Holomisa took control of the homeland in a coup d'état in 1987.

The most stressful trips were to Lusaka, since it took up to four days and involved travelling in the middle of the night and a lot of waiting at various meeting points in different countries. On one such trip in the late 1980s, I first had to meet up with a contact in Swartruggens who was responsible for my passage through the border post near Zeerust. On the South African side everything went according to plan, but when I got to the Botswana side the designated contact wasn't there and I didn't have the correct papers.

I panicked, as missing the appointment with my contact had several practical consequences and would set into motion a chain reaction from Gaborone to Lusaka. For starters, I would not have a place to stay in Gaborone because I didn't have any money to book into a hotel.

Also, most hotels were monitored by the South African Police's Security Branch. I could not risk being stuck in Gaborone for days with no place to stay.

The rule was that if something went wrong, for instance if one person in a specific chain went missing, then everyone up the chain had to make a move in case that person was caught by the Security Branch. If the police then forced a confession out of him, it put the lives of everyone involved at risk.

Although I had a telephone number for someone in Botswana, the public phones were out of order that evening. Fortunately, my contact from Gaborone, a smart Indian comrade, suspected that something might have gone wrong and he sent a Batswana resident to use his influence at the border to get me passage. It was a huge relief when I finally managed to clear the border a few hours later.

South African security forces had raided several ANC safe houses in Gaborone the previous week and a number of ANC cadres had been killed. When I got to Gaborone, my contact told me I had to leave for Lusaka that very night as enemy agents were still in town and he believed our lives were in danger. I was bundled into a vehicle and driven to what appeared to be a remote private airstrip and flown out of Botswana to Harare and then on to Lusaka.

On these trips to Lusaka I met several ANC leaders, including Thabo Mbeki, Alfred Nzo, Thomas Nkobi, Pallo Jordan and Joel Netshitenzhe. Joel, whose nom de guerre was Peter Mayibuye, was always part of the Youth Section delegation, and was warm and soft-spoken. At that time he wore his hair in an Afro and had a beard – he really looked the part of a revolutionary. His contributions to meetings were always insightful, and he struck me as deep thinker and a well-read individual. Even though he believed in a certain level of militancy, he was never the type to raise his voice.

While I had heard many good things about Jacob Zuma and idolised him as one of the top ANC leaders, I never met him in Lusaka in the

1980s or in the early 1990s when many ANC leaders returned to the country. People I knew who had contact with Zuma in exile always told me how he was one of the most accessible and down-to-earth leaders. He was also known for making time to meet people who had just left the country to go into exile, and those who reported to him have fond memories of him as a compassionate and accessible leader who was always on hand to give advice when needed. Those who worked with after his return from exile had the same impression.

The 1980s were a tense and dangerous time as the apartheid state tried to clamp down on the rising discontent and revolt by the black majority. Protest marches were the order of the day and the security forces became increasingly violent in their response to the unrest.

The first state of emergency was declared in 1985. It heightened the powers of the South African Defence Force and the South African Police and gave the state the power to detain political activists without trial. More organisations were banned and many activists were detained for up to three or four years without seeing the inside of a courtroom. Activists were abducted from their homes by the security forces and their bodies were later found in open fields. I spent many weekends attending funerals of activists who had been abducted or killed during the various protests in different parts of the country.

As student leaders of Azaso/Sansco, our task was to mobilise young people, particularly students in tertiary education, to join the struggle against apartheid. We organised various political campaigns, which included class boycotts, protest marches and mass student gatherings on campuses. Azaso/Sansco was the largest and most popular student organisation at tertiary institutions throughout the country and was affiliated to the UDF. We mounted a number of actions in support of UDF campaigns, including the demand to release Mandela and other political prisoners, and the unbanning of the liberation movements. This made the organisation a target of the security forces.

Leading a protest at Wits for the unbanning of the
United Democratic Front (UDF). (Credit: Arena Holdings)

Universities, especially black universities, became hotbeds of political activity, and the regime even deployed the army to suppress student action. At one point the Turfloop campus of the University of the North (today the University of Limpopo) was occupied by the South African Defence Force for months, with student leaders being subjected to prolonged periods of detention without trial.

The security forces often raided Glen Thomas House, and many of my comrades were detained without trial for many months. Friends such as Chris Ngcobo, who would go on to become the chief of the Johannesburg Metro Police, and Pascal Moloi, later Johannesburg city manager, were among the student leaders detained without trial for more than three years. The security forces kept tabs on all of us, and despite our best efforts to remain under the radar, they knew about many of our activities.

In later years Moloi told me that he had been interrogated about a meeting I had had in Geneva, Switzerland, with Trevor Abrahams, an exiled ANC member, during one of my overseas trips. Abrahams was working at the offices of the World University Service and was a key ANC contact person in Geneva. He assisted me in making contact with sister student organisations that were part of the global anti-apartheid movement in Europe.

I survived these raids largely due to my underground training, first in the SACP and later in the ANC. I was taught never to sleep in one place for two nights in a row. After having dinner and socialising with friends and comrades at Glen Thomas House, I would sneak out to spend the night either at the home of a close friend from school, who stayed at a residence in Parktown, or at the home of one of the white student activists. When I did spend the night at Glen Thomas House, I never slept in my own room. Constantly feeling unsafe brought on a kind of pressure that was unbearable to many activists, who faced the risk of detention on a daily basis.

The apartheid regime became more and more desperate as international pressure mounted to unban political organisations and release Nelson Mandela and other political leaders. In early 1985, President PW Botha announced that he would release Mandela on certain conditions, including that Mandela and the ANC renounce violence.

In February 1985 the UDF held a rally at the Jabulani Amphitheatre in Soweto to celebrate Archbishop Desmond Tutu's receiving the Nobel Peace Prize. Thousands of people attended, including dignitaries from various embassies. I was on the speakers' list that day and sat on the stage with the rest of the UDF leadership. It was a hot summer's day and the crowd was singing and chanting – the atmosphere was electric. When the MC called me to the podium he told me I only had one minute since there were many organisations and VIPs who wanted a turn to speak.

I was disappointed but also relieved, because I was quite overwhelmed. I managed to shout a few slogans into the microphone: 'Viva

ANC, Viva UDF, Viva Azaso, Viva Cosas, long live Mandela!' I could have been arrested on the spot and sent to Robben Island for mentioning the ANC in public.

The next moment, the beautiful and militant Zindzi Mandela went to the podium, to a roar from the crowd. In his brilliance, Mandela had written a letter to his daughter in which he set out the reasons for not accepting the government's conditions for his release. Although seemingly addressed to her, it was in fact a statement to the nation and the rest of the world.

In the conclusion Mandela said: 'Only free men can negotiate, prisoners cannot enter into contracts. Herman Toivo ya Toivo, when freed, never gave any undertaking, nor was he called upon to do so. I cannot and will not give any undertaking at this time when I and you, the

*Making a speech at
a UDF protest meeting
at Wits in August 1987.*
(Credit: Arena Holdings)

people are not free. Your freedom and mine cannot be separated. I will return.'

Young and old jumped up and down, crying and ululating. For the first time in decades, Madiba had spoken directly to us through his very brave daughter. I had goosebumps all over my body.

The campaign for Mandela's release gained momentum locally and internationally. Aubrey Mokoena, a UDF activist from Soweto, took particular interest in this effort. This led to the formation of the Release Mandela Campaign, which ran the campaign in South Africa. I was recruited to the campaign and became part of its programmes and activities.

In 1986 the Release Mandela Campaign was renamed the Mandela Reception Committee and we started raising funds from foreign governments and non-governmental organisations to prepare for Mandela's release. The Reception Committee was made up of prominent leaders of the MDM and became one of the first organisations inside the country to produce media (T-shirts and pamphlets) with Mandela's face printed on them. This was in total defiance of the security laws, which forbade anyone from publishing a photo of him.

Of course, my studies suffered under my intense involvement in struggle politics. Some years I only attended about ten per cent of my lectures, but I tried to catch up whenever I could. Fortunately, fellow activists also shared their class notes with me.

Another consequence of my political activities was that I had little time to attend family gatherings, weddings and funerals. I had become a child of the struggle and my comrades became my new family. My parents were very unhappy that they saw so little of me. Sometimes months would pass without my visiting the family home in Dube.

On the afternoon of 29 August 1986 I returned to Glen Thomas House from campus. I was feeling pretty tired, but something told me to phone home and check how my mother was doing. No one answered my call, which was unusual, so I decided to go to Dube.

When I got to our house there was no one there, so I spoke to a neighbour who told me that my mother was unwell and that my brothers had taken her to Baragwanath Hospital.

I rushed to the hospital, where I found two of my brothers sleeping in our father's car in the parking area outside the casualty ward. They told me that my mother had experienced bleeding from the nose for most of the day and had collapsed around 2 pm. They had to wait in a long queue before they could get her admitted to the hospital.

I struggled to get the attention of the nurses who were running around trying to attend to the vast number of casualties. Eventually, a nurse checked the admission list and took me to the ward where my mother had been taken. The nurse in charge of the ward gave me a stern look. 'Follow me,' she said.

The hospital was incredibly overcrowded, with beds in the passages and some patients lying on mattresses on the floor. The next moment the nurse entered a ward and walked towards a bed around which white plastic curtains had been pulled. She opened the curtain, went inside and didn't say a word before she emerged again a few seconds later.

By then, I was struggling to breathe due to the stench of blood in the ward. The nurse looked at the file and asked what my relationship was to the patient. 'I am her son,' I said anxiously. She asked if I was alone or with someone else. My heart started beating very fast. 'Could I just see my mother, please?'

She moved aside and opened the curtains. There my mother was, with her eyes closed and her mouth wide open, a bloodstain on her neck. She had a deep gash just above her breast and there was a tube stuck inside the hole. Another tube was still in her mouth.

I had no control over the tears that starting rolling from my eyes. I walked closer and touched her cold hand and face. My mother was dead. According to the death certificate she had died of a stroke induced by excessive blood loss.

I realised then that I had not seen or spoken to my mother for about three months. It wasn't because I didn't care but because I had been so caught up in my political work. In that moment I was confronted with so many questions: did she know that I loved her? Was she proud of me? Did she know that she could have come to my residence for help?

I felt terrible for not being there when she died. To this day I regret it.

The walk from the ward to the car was probably the longest in my life. I broke the news to my brothers, who were still waiting in the car. My father had not yet returned from work and we couldn't reach him by phone. When my old man finally got home around 11 pm and heard of my mother's passing, he broke down. Seeing my father cry hit me hard, as I had never seen him in tears before.

As a young man, you know that no one lives for ever, but you cling to the illusion that your parents will always be there for you. I learnt early on that you cannot take your parents for granted.

By the late 1980s, the struggle had intensified and there was greater coordination between what the ANC was doing in exile and what we were doing internally as the MDM under the banner of the UDF. This took the form of a Defiance Campaign that led to more and more activists being arrested, with some dying in detention and many leaving the country.

Major anti-apartheid protests were held outside South African embassies abroad, an international sports boycott was beginning to bite and an economic sanctions campaign was gaining momentum, with more and more countries beginning to force their companies to divest from South Africa. The armed struggle was also on the rise in many parts of the country. All of these constituted what we called the 'four pillars' of the struggle, namely, internal mass mobilisation, armed propaganda/struggle, international isolation and building and strengthening the underground structures of the ANC.

Visiting my friend, Vhonani Mufamadi (not pictured),
at his home in Meadowlands, Soweto.

I had to spend more time in hiding as more and more activists were being killed by the security forces. Every day became a struggle for survival and I began to feel a great sense of despair. The nights became my new enemy as I struggled to sleep. I had to watch my movements carefully; it seemed like death was knocking at my door.

The regime used all manner of tactics to get rid of activists, including assassinations, killings in detention, mass shootings during demonstrations and turning activists into agents provocateurs to get comrades to kill one another. For instance, at a funeral the security forces would use agents provocateurs to accuse an activist of being a spy and get the crowd to attack that person. This often led to the infamous and brutal necklace killings in which a tyre was placed around the neck of

43

the alleged spy, doused with petrol and set alight. We lost a few activists in this way. I was warned by my superiors in the underground
to be selective about the funerals I attended and never to attend a
funeral alone.

One of the people I met as a young activist at Wits was Bheki
Mlangeni, a feisty and streetwise activist from Jabulani, in Soweto,
who was studying law at Wits and also stayed at Glen Thomas House.
I couldn't help but notice his pantsula dress code; you would always

Bheki Mlangeni at his home
in Jabulani, Soweto.
(Credit: Arena Holdings)

see him in chino trousers, with either shiny shoes or white Converse
takkies. I first met Bheki when I joined the Azaso branch at Wits in
1984, and he immediately struck me as a very dedicated and thought-
ful member of the organisation. He was friendly but very strict when
it came to performing organisational tasks, and I soon realised he was
a go-to person on all organisational matters.

I respected Bheki for his discipline and his legal mind. Although he
shied away from or rejected any suggestion that he should assume a
leadership position, he was a great influence on the rest of us, and we
considered him a struggle mentor. He became like a brother to me
because he always provided emotional support in difficult times and

never hesitated to give advice about the academic and personal challenges I faced.

In 1985 Bheki was detained and held at Diepkloof prison, also known as Sun City, for a few months. After he completed his degree, he did his legal articles at Cheadle Thompson & Haysom, a progressive law firm based in Jorrison Street, Braamfontein. Bheki had promised that he would ensure that I got to do my articles at the firm once I finished my Bachelor of Laws (LLB). I suspect that this was his way of making sure I continued with my studies and stayed in the country, because I had hinted to him that I was considering going into exile to receive military training. His view was that not all of us had to go into exile as there was still a lot of political work to be done inside the country.

In 1988 I seriously considered going into exile. Although Bheki initially discouraged me, he subsequently supported my decision to go. It was a difficult decision, which came with great risk. While I still had ambitions of becoming an advocate, and of using the law to fight the injustices of colonialism and apartheid, I was also very angry at that time and felt I had to leave.

However, I worried about letting my father down as I was supposed to be the child who would break the cycle of poverty in my family. I had a steady girlfriend, Phindile Dlamini, solid friendships and a strong bond with members of my extended family. To make matters worse, I could not tell any of my friends or family members of my plans, so it was also a lonely journey.

I discussed my plans with five comrades – Bheki, Lawrence Boya, Chris Ngcobo, Sancho (whose surname I cannot remember) and Dreyfus Thotela, a feisty and very militant comrade from the Free State. We finally agreed that Lawrence, Dreyfus, Sancho and I would leave the country. We started making plans and appointed comrade Louis Thabo Mohale, another student activist from Vista University in Soweto, to make the logistical arrangements.

One day in early 1988, we left Johannesburg and travelled to the

Ramatlabama border post north of Mafikeng (today Mahikeng). About a kilometre from the border gate, Louis stopped and pointed to a gravel road that went past the border post. He instructed us to walk on the gravel until we were over the border, and said someone would meet us on the Botswana side. As we walked along the border fence, we suspected something was amiss as we noticed armed soldiers who had clearly spotted us.

As we approached the place where we were supposed to jump the fence, a group of heavily armed soldiers approached us and arrested us on the spot. They had apparently been waiting for us. We tried to turn back, but it was too late. We were arrested, loaded into the back of a police van and taken to what appeared to be the makeshift offices of the Security Branch in the Old Mutual building in Swartruggens. There we were detained, interrogated and severely beaten for about three days.

The interrogation rooms, which doubled as sleeping quarters, were on either the fifth or sixth floor of the building and were dimly lit, with small windows that couldn't open. I hated the fact that my interrogators always smoked in the room, especially after I told them I was a non-smoker.

The policemen would arrive in the morning with a pen and paper and ask me to write down my biography, including the details of all my family members and our ANC contacts inside and outside the country. They would collect the papers a few hours later. On their return, they would handcuff me behind my back – I was made to sit on a metal chair – and begin with the daily routine of aggressive interrogation. They hit me all over my body and even kicked me in my private parts.

The interrogation took most of the day, with lunch breaks (for them) in between. At one point I began to doubt if I would make it out alive. Part of me was glad I was handcuffed; otherwise, I might have fought back, which could have had dire consequences. That is exactly how

Steve Biko lost his life, because he fought back and his interrogators outnumbered and killed him.

Before we left Johannesburg, Lawrence had suggested that if we were caught, we should use the cover story that we were leaving the country because we wanted to go and study overseas. Although Lawrence, Sancho, Dreyfus and I were kept and interrogated in separate rooms, the Security Branch members made sure that we heard one another's screams during the beatings. They would do the well-known 'good cop, bad cop' routine and claim that my comrades were already telling the truth and that I should do the same.

Thankfully, none of us gave in. We stuck to our story that we were trying to leave the country to go and study overseas.

I feared for my life because these thugs could have done anything to us and no one knew where we were. Bear in mind that this was not a formal police station where records of our arrest would be kept.

After about three days we were taken to the Protea police station in Soweto. We were locked in the cells for about three weeks and interrogated further by local members of the Security Branch. The interrogation was as intensive as before, and included the same methods of getting us to write down the details of our background, plans, ANC contact persons in Gaborone and our activities in the student movement. Then one day we were released without being charged.

We returned to our normal activist lives with dented egos, deeply disappointed that our effort to join Umkhonto we Sizwe, the ANC's military wing, had failed.

The following year, in February 1989, I had another brush with death when the security forces hatched a plan to assassinate a number of student leaders from Sansco and Cosas.

One day I received a call from Louis Mohale, who had been involved in our effort to go into exile and who was also one of the Sansco leaders in the Transvaal region. He informed me that he had been approached by the ANC in exile to bring a delegation to Swaziland (today Eswatini) for an urgent meeting between Sansco and the ANC Youth Section. Another Sansco executive member who received an instruction to go on the trip was Thula Ngcobo from the Medical University of South Africa (Medunsa).

Louis didn't seem to be aware that I was one of the few people designated as a link between the ANC and the Azaso/Sansco at the time. His call struck me as unusual because such a request would normally have come directly to me or one of the designated contact persons in the organisation. What made the message even stranger was that it came as more of an instruction than a request and we were only given a few days' notice to travel to Swaziland.

Communicating with the ANC in Lusaka was not always easy, and I spent days trying to make contact with my people in Lusaka, Lesotho and Botswana, but I couldn't verify the legitimacy of this instruction. The date for the meeting was fast approaching, but I felt uncomfortable telling Louis that we didn't trust his process, so I tried to convince him to postpone the meeting. He refused, however, and insisted that it go ahead.

I spent many hours on the phone with Thula discussing the trip, and we finally agreed not to go. In our opinion, it was not authorised. The meeting was scheduled for a Saturday morning, and on that day I happened to be on a rare visit to my parents' home in Dube. At around 7 am, Louis and two guys unexpectedly arrived at the house, ostensibly to pick me up for the trip. I was very surprised, as I had already told him I would not be going. Furthermore, I had not told him I would be at my parents' home that morning.

I told him that even if I wanted to, I couldn't go, as I didn't have a passport. I became very suspicious when he pulled out a document that was purportedly my passport. He insisted that I call Thula and another activist from Wits to tell them we were on our way to fetch them. I politely told him that we were not going anywhere. It helped that their car was blocking that of my father; he was getting impatient because he wanted to leave. When he came out of the house to tell them to move the car, they must have thought he was chasing them away, because they simply drove off.

Sadly, Louis had apparently convinced Sansco members Portia Shabangu and Derek Mashobane to go on the trip, and the three of them drove to Swaziland. According to the report of the Truth and Reconciliation Commission (TRC), they were told to meet their contact in the Swazi Plaza in Mbabane.[3] Louis's contact turned out to be an askari – an ANC member who had switched sides to join the police – who lured them into an ambush point in a secluded forest area near Bhunya, where they were shot and killed by members of the South African security forces. Approximately ten operatives participated in the ambush, two of whom were askaris.[4]

A few days later, we received news reports that three South African students had been killed in Swaziland when a car was ambushed by the security forces. The car described in the report matched the one Louis had used when he visited my parents' house. When I subsequently managed to make contact with my connection in Lusaka, he confirmed that the ANC had never requested the meeting in Swaziland.

In the TRC report it was revealed that Louis, Portia and Derek were killed by a Vlakplaas squad under the command of Captain Eugene de Kock in an operation code-named Cobra. According to De Kock's submission to the TRC, Operation Cobra was intended to eliminate 15 to 16 student leaders of Sansco and Cosas.[5]

The news of the murders affected me very badly, and for the first time I really feared for my life. I was advised by my contacts to lie low. I was deeply depressed that I could not attend the funerals of the three fallen students. Several years later, when De Kock and his former colleagues testified before the TRC and applied for amnesty, I could not muster enough courage to attend the hearings.

4

South Africa gets a black president

ON 18 JANUARY 1989, President PW Botha suffered a stroke, and about two weeks later FW de Klerk was elected leader of the ruling National Party. When De Klerk became president of the country in August that year, he hinted that he was considering the release of Nelson Mandela and other political leaders, as well as unbanning all political parties, on condition that they renounce violence as a strategy.

On 2 February 1990, I was on a regional visit to campuses in Durban and surrounding areas in my capacity as general secretary of Sansco. That day, at the official opening of Parliament, De Klerk announced that Mandela would be released. I and many of my comrades were caught completely off-guard; even though we knew the release was imminent, we did not expect it to happen that soon.

Mandela was released on 11 February and we watched on television as he walked out of Victor Verster prison (today Drakenstein Correctional Centre), outside Paarl. After 27 years in jail, the tall and handsome Madiba emerged wearing a grey suit and somewhat dated spectacles, and holding the hand of his wife, Winnie. I would have given anything to be there in person. My fellow comrades who were with me burst into tears and started jumping up and down. Most of us had never thought we would live to see our leader released from prison.

The moment we had fought for all our lives had arrived and an important milestone in our struggle had been reached.

When Mandela was released in 1990, the Reception Committee was assigned the task of managing part of his political programme, including coordinating international trips to countries that had supported our anti-apartheid struggle in general and the Release Mandela Campaign in particular. The only international trip I participated in was to Namibia to meet with the South West Africa People's Organisation and attend the ceremonies marking Namibian independence.

One of my favourite memories of that trip is how, as we were about to board the plane to go home, President Sam Nujoma and his comrades wished Madiba a safe flight. Madiba's unthinking response was 'Same to you, comrades,' as if they were also about to go on a trip. I laughed all the way to my seat.

Welcoming ANC stalwart Govan Mbeki (right) at an AZASO conference after his release from Robben Island.

By the late 1980s, we realised that victory over the apartheid regime was within reach and we started having discussions about what should happen when the regime fell. In 1988, the National Education Co-ordinating Committee (NECC) approached education policy units at various universities around the country and eventually launched a research project that became known as the National Education Policy Investigation.

Research working groups were established to investigate topics such as access, early childhood educare, adult basic education, education policy systems, support services, etc. I joined the Wits Education Policy Unit to lead the education law workstream, which looked at all the apartheid education laws that a new government would have to re-move from the statute books.

In 1991 high school education went through another crisis, with the possibility that students would not write the end-of-year exams. Various meetings were held between the NECC, the de facto education de-partment for black South Africans, and Stoffel van der Merwe, then minister of education and training. Sadly, these meetings yielded no results due to the minister's intransigence.

After the NECC met with Mandela and other ANC leaders, it was agreed that the ANC should convene an urgent meeting between the NECC and Van der Merwe. Thabo Mbeki was assigned the task of facilitating the meeting. I had met Mbeki and some of the other lead-ers a few times before, but I was always a little nervous when I was in their company. I idolised them. Mbeki always stood out because he smoked a pipe and because of his insightful contributions to any dis-cussion. As a young activist, I used to hang on his every word.

Van der Merwe happened to be in Cape Town at that time, so we had to fly there. Mandela spoke to some businesspeople and asked them to make a private jet available as it was a matter of urgency that we get to Cape Town that evening.

I had never been on a private jet before. Just imagine: here was I, a laaitie from Dube, travelling on a private jet with Thabo Mbeki, discussing how we were going to approach a meeting with an apartheid Cabinet minister. Mbeki lit his pipe several times during the flight, as smoking was still allowed on planes. I noticed that he had forgotten to shave, something that turned out to be quite characteristic of him and that we eventually got used to.

I was asked to give my view on the root cause of the crisis and how I thought we should approach the meeting with the minister. Essentially, my view was that we should not compromise on the students' demands, which included the provision of free textbooks, the building of more schools to relieve overcrowding and the release of student leaders from detention. Mbeki then went on to give us his perspective on the crisis, its relevance to the overall struggle and how it should be managed. I listened enraptured.

During our discussions, the flight attendants offered us drinks and snacks. Mbeki and the other leaders drank whisky but I stuck to soft drinks, pretending to be teetotal. I was amazed that an entire bottle of whisky was reunited with its ancestors during the short flight to Cape Town and another one on the flight back. I was pleased when they also served supper because I was very hungry. However, I was terribly disappointed by the size of the portions.

We arrived in Cape Town around 9 pm and went straight to the meeting in the minister's office in the parliamentary precinct. Mbeki presented our side of the story in the most eloquent way imaginable. Van der Merwe seemed uncomfortable and unable to provide a cogent response.

In the end, all our demands were met, so for us the meeting ended well.

Friday 15 February 1991 started out as a normal day, but would end up being one of the most painful days of my life. I went to campus to try and catch up with my classes before taking the afternoon bus back to Glen Thomas House. I was exhausted from all my commitments and took a nap, but around 6 pm I was woken up by a loud knock on my door.

'There's an urgent call for you,' said the person on the other side of the door.

I rushed to the reception area, where there were public telephone booths. I noticed that a few of my comrades were standing around, looking upset. I picked up the phone.

'Themba, you need to come. Something terrible has happened to Bheki.'

On the line was a relative of my dear friend and mentor Bheki Mlangeni. A group of us immediately got into my car and rushed to Bheki's family home in Jabulani. No one said a single word on the 10-kilometre trip. We were too scared even to speculate about what could have happened. As we approached the house, we saw that people had gathered outside the gate.

Bheki's home was a typical four-roomed township house, where he lived with his mother and other siblings. He was married to his long-time girlfriend, Sepati, and they had a son.

Bheki had managed to save some money, and had worked with his mother to build on a few external rooms, where he stayed with his wife.

When we got out of the car all I could hear was loud screams emanating from inside the house. The yard was packed with neighbours, activists and friends. I was shaking with fear. We greeted and shook hands with those we could make eye contact with. On my way into the house, I bumped into one of Bheki's relatives.

'They've killed him,' she said and started sobbing uncontrollably.

As I forced my body to move towards Bheki's room, a large lump grew in my throat. Part of me said, don't go in there, but there was no turning back. I went in, but what I saw made me recoil in horror. Mabhekzin's lifeless body was lying on the bed, but half of his head was gone. Blown off. There was blood everywhere – on the floor, the ceiling, the walls, the curtains, the blankets, the books, the wardrobe doors. Everything seemed to be covered in red splatters.

I wanted to get closer and touch him but the old man who was waiting inside prevented me. I don't know why I had this urge to get closer, possibly because I couldn't see his face and part of me thought, or wished, that maybe it was not him. Maybe they had made a mistake, just maybe . . .

Everything else that happened after that moment is a blur. Bheki was dead. He had been murdered a few metres from his mother, his son and his fiancée. I would never hear his soft voice again.

The previous year, Bheki had been involved with an investigation into the death squads operated by the apartheid security forces, after former police captain Dirk Coetzee made certain revelations about the activities of the Civil Cooperation Bureau and other units. Legal firm Cheadle Thompson & Haysom presented evidence to the Harms Commission of Inquiry into the activities of the South African Defence Force and South African Police counterinsurgency units.[6] During this time, Bheki had several direct dealings with Coetzee, who supplied key testimony to the Harms Commission.

Eugene de Kock, who headed the death squad at Vlakplaas, wanted to assassinate Coetzee and sent him a parcel containing a booby-trapped Walkman cassette player and tapes to a postal address in Zambia, where Coetzee was in hiding at the time. The earphones contained an explosive device. The sender's name was given as Bheki Mlangeni and the return address was that of his law firm. The parcel was never collected, however, and consequently was sent back to South Africa. According to Sepati's testimony to the TRC, the parcel was marked 'Evidence, hit squad'. They were in their room at home when Bheki put on the earphones, which exploded the moment he pressed the play button.[7]

Bheki was 35 when he was murdered and had a very promising legal career ahead of him. I often wonder what would have happened if he hadn't been killed. Perhaps he would have been a judge today.

By this time we were constantly listening to the news bulletins, expecting to hear about the killing or disappearance of an activist almost on a daily basis. But Mabhekzin's death hit many of us hard. He had mentored, guided and advised so many of us, and also reprimanded and threatened to beat us up if we were ill-disciplined. There were a few times when I came very close to getting a hot klap from him for doing this or that. Mabhekzin was not just a comrade; he was a spiritual leader, a brother and a father to so many of us. We both respected and feared him.

Part of me realised that it could have been me that night. His loss is a pain I carry to this day.

I was elated when, in 2014, the Gauteng provincial government named a new hospital in Jabulani the Bheki Mlangeni District Hospital. A community park was also named after him, and the Bheki Mlangeni Foundation has been established to initiate a number of projects, including a memorial lecture and a bursary fund, to keep his memory alive.

The year 1991 did not only bring sorrow, though. By that time I had been in a relationship with the beautiful Phindile Dlamini for six years. Phindi was born in Soweto and grew up initially in Zola before her family moved to White City, Jabavu. She attended Bopasenatla Secondary School, in Diepkloof, Soweto, which was next to Immaculata High School. Phindile was a devout Christian with very strong values of honesty, hard work and respect for humanity in general. Most of all, though, she had a beautiful smile, which brightened my day from a distance, and I loved her long dark hair. I had been looking at and admiring her from a distance but lacked the courage to make the first move until I got lucky and found an empty seat next to her in the bus after school. Although I had dated before, my feelings for Phindile were different and something inside told me that this was something special. We dated for six years before we decided to get married.

Left: *In Meadow-lands with my then girlfriend, Phindi, who is now my wife.* Bottom: *During our wedding celebration in Sandton in 1991.*

Our wedding was rather unconventional. A white wedding was not our thing, and we agreed that we would rather use the little cash we had to buy our first house. Since we expected our families to protest against the fact that we didn't want a big traditional wedding with many guests, we made the bold move of not inviting any friends or family. Although Phindi had suggested that we invite our parents, and she informed her mother of our plans, I was not keen because I didn't want parents to complicate things. I knew that my father would insist on a typical township wedding with all the bells and whistles, and I wasn't up for that. As an activist, I had witnessed many weddings in the township, including that of my elder brother, and I wasn't keen to go through the experience of dressing up, dancing in the street and spending loads of cash to feed mouths who had nothing to do with my future family.

One of my best friends from Immaculata High School, Neo Tladinyana, arranged for a priest, Dr Seth Molefe Pitikoe, to preside over our marriage at the Catholic church in Tladi, and we set the date for 27 April 1991. I was still actively involved in my political work and had meetings that day. The problem with these meetings was that they never finished on time, so I had asked Neo to fetch Phindi from the apartment and take her to the church. In other words, I was late for my own wedding!

When I got to the church, the priest asked if anyone else, such as our parents, was on their way, and I confidently told him that he should proceed, as no one else was coming. All I can say is that we've been happily married for 30 years, despite all the naysayers who told us at the time that our marriage would never last because we did not follow any tradition. All Phindi and I knew was that we were madly in love and wanted to start a family and spend the rest of our lives together.

Needless to say, it was very difficult letting our parents know that we had tied the knot in their absence. When I told my father we were already married, he was furious and threatened to report me to his brothers and the rest of the extended family. But I was young and rebellious and the threat of appearing before a family gathering did not bother me.

I sat him down, apologised profusely and told him that we preferred to buy a house rather than throw a party. What really saved the day was that he knew and adored Phindi. He had accepted her as his makoti (family bride) the day I introduced her to him. He forgave us, blessed the marriage and went on to become our spiritual guide.

At the time, Phindi was working as a marketing professional at Hewlett-Packard, a computer company. Her boss was not impressed with us for not having a proper wedding celebration, and she arranged a small dinner party for us at the company offices in Sandton. I reluctantly agreed and we partied with some of Phindi's work colleagues in one of their entertainment areas.

After accepting the fait accompli of our marriage, my father agreed to assist us with part of the deposit to purchase our first home in Kempton Park, on the East Rand. At the time this was a lower-middle-class, white and Afrikaans neighbourhood. We were the first black family to move into the area, and for a few months we lived there in defiance of the Group Areas Act, which was only repealed at the end of June 1991. Our white neighbours hated the idea that they had black neighbours, but we didn't give a chicken's wing about that. We hosted many parties and even slaughtered a live animal or two during family gatherings.

Our marriage was blessed with two intelligent and handsome boys. Our first child was born in April 1992, and we named him Thabo to symbolise the joy and happiness that his arrival brought to our marriage. Our second son, Nqobi, was born in April 1995.

One of the regrets I have about my life is that I never spent enough time with my kids. I am forever grateful to Phindi for sacrificing her career for the sake of our young family. Phindi's job at Hewlett-Packard, as manager in charge of small business development, also involved a

*A rare moment of family time with my sons Nqobi (left) and
Thabo (right) in 1997.*

lot of local and overseas travel, and we did not have the privilege of
having support for our two sons. My work schedule kept me away
from home for prolonged periods of time, especially later, during my
stint as government spokesperson. There would even be times when
we had issues about who would fetch the kids from school. I regret that
I was not as present in my sons' lives as a father should be.

In retrospect, history repeated itself: my father was always working
late and never had the opportunity to set foot in any of my schools
when I was a kid. My kids suffered the same fate from me. Those of us
who work hard to be of service to the nation often commit the mistake of putting our country before our families, and fail, sometimes
dismally, to strike a balance between the two. With the benefit of hindsight, activists should do more to achieve this balance. For instance,
during my years as director-general and government spokesperson I
used to come home with a stack of files of 'submissions' (for my sig-
nature) as my homework instead of using evenings to catch up with

my boys and my wife. It was possible for me to do that, but I was too focused on getting the job done. In the process I neglected my family.

In 1993 I also finally graduated from Wits University with a Bachelor of Arts (BA) degree and an LLB. By then I was working as assistant general secretary of the NECC on a full-time basis. I had the qualifications to realise my dream of becoming an attorney or an advocate. At Wits I learnt much, both academically and politically. I also learnt a great deal in the corridors and on the lawns of the university.

In the 1980s life for a black student at Wits was no bed of roses, as Bantu Education did not prepare us sufficiently for university. We made up less than five per cent of the student population and most of us had transport and accommodation issues and no support from the university. Those of us who were fortunate might have a Chelsea bun and some water as our lunch, but many of our black brothers and sisters spent the whole day on campus without any meals.

My late father (right) and my wife, Phindi, attending my LLB graduation ceremony at Wits.

Our struggles with the university authorities bore fruit as we got them to meet many of our demands through protest action. Some of the victories included forcing the university to find accommodation for poor black students, introducing the Academic Support Programme. We also forced the university to allow workers to establish the National Education, Health and Allied Workers' Union (Nehawu) and used our connections to help the workers affiliate to the Congress of South African Trade Unions.

I also learnt a lot about alliance politics, which enabled me to participate in the process of getting all student organisations and societies, academics and sports associations on campus to join our protests against apartheid and to support our many demands, including the release of Nelson Mandela and other political prisoners, the unbanning of student organisations and the lifting of the various state of emergency regulations.

I participated in several protest marches and spent many nights in John Vorster Square police station after being arrested. I also led many delegations to present student demands to the university administration, including accommodation for black students and the readmission of students excluded for failing to pay fees or for not meeting the academic requirements. When the #FeesMustFall movement first took off in 2015, it really resonated with me.

I owe a lot of who I am today to the hundreds of activists who were members of Azaso, Sansco and NUSAS. I learnt more about life from my interactions with them than from the many lectures I attended.

In December 1991 the formal negotiations to bring an end to apartheid started with the Convention for a Democratic South Africa (Codesa). The ANC and the National Party were the two largest and most influential players during these talks, which led to the country's first-ever democratic elections in April 1994.

On 10 April 1993 tragedy hit when Chris Hani, the much-loved commander of Umkhonto we Sizwe, the ANC's military wing, and leader of the SACP, was assassinated outside his house in Dawn Park, a suburb of Boksburg, on the East Rand. Hani had gone to the shops to buy a Sunday newspaper, and as he walked back to his house he was shot a few metres from his front door. His killing brought South Africa to the brink of civil war, as it was soon established that he had been shot by a Polish right-winger, aided by a Conservative Party politician.

Pictures of Hani's lifeless body lying on the ground made headlines around the world. I was devastated, as I had met him on several occasions in Lusaka and he had made a great impression on me. As the most prominent commander of Umkhonto we Sizwe, Hani was militant and committed to advancing the armed struggle against the apartheid regime. I was inspired by his tough language in reference to the National Party government. After the SACP was unbanned, I was elected to the Transvaal Interim Provincial Committee of the SACP and attended a few meetings with Hani at his office in the Johannesburg city centre. He always came across as very strict and intolerant of activists who missed meetings, arrived late or failed to perform their tasks diligently. Even if this made me a little scared of stepping out of line, it made me respect him. I never dared to arrive late to any meeting I knew he would be attending.

After Hani's murder, the ruling National Party's call for calm fell on deaf ears. The only reason why we as young activists didn't rise up was because of Nelson Mandela's address on national television on 13 April. He pleaded with the nation to calm down and assured everyone that he would ensure that Hani's killers were found and sent to jail for a long time. Mandela spoke to the nation as if he was already president, and the nation listened. Fortunately, Hani's killers were apprehended within days, largely thanks to an eyewitness who reported the incident to the police.

In the months leading up to the 1994 elections, political parties started compiling lists of their representatives for national and provincial legislatures. The political settlement reached at Codesa included dividing the country into nine provinces, each with its own government. The ANC had one of the most democratic processes for selecting candidates for its parliamentary list, as it invited sectoral organisations that were part of the anti-apartheid struggle, such as civics and trade unions, to nominate individuals for inclusion in the electoral list. As a member of the national executive of the NECC, I was nominated to represent the education constituency. I was number 270 on the ANC list.

While everyone knew the ANC would win the elections decisively, it wasn't a given that it would get enough votes for someone who was number 270 on the list to go to Parliament. Our assessment at the time was that only those who were between 1 and 250 on the electoral list were guaranteed a seat. However, when the 1994 election results were announced, it became clear that it was a landslide victory for the ANC. At age 30, I would become one of the youngest Members of Parliament (MP).

I joined the celebrations with the many ANC activists who had worked hard to campaign for the party. That same evening, my wife and I called my father to inform him that I would be going to Parliament as an MP. Although he was elated at the good news, I could tell from his voice that he didn't fully understand what it entailed. The next day, we went to visit him in order to tell him more about my immediate future. All he wanted to know was who would be paying for my trip to Cape Town, where I would be staying and how long I would be in the city.

I took time to explain everything to him in detail, including that Parliament would cover my travel and accommodation costs. He was all smiles when I told him that I would sit in Parliament with the likes of Madiba and other ANC leaders. He gave me his blessings, said a little prayer and wished me well.

On the day we were to be sworn in as new MPs, a bunch of us were bundled onto an early-morning South African Airways (SAA) flight to Cape Town. Although this was not my first flight to Cape Town, it was the first time I was on a flight where the majority of the passengers were black. I suspect it must have come as something of a culture shock to the white passengers, as we were not quiet travellers. We had just won a major electoral victory and the fact of being on an aircraft did not prevent us from singing our struggle songs.

When we arrived at the parliamentary precinct, we were treated like VIPs: everything was 'sir' this and 'sir' that. The parliamentary staff, the majority of whom were white at that time, must have been briefed well.

The registration process took for ever and reminded some of us of the process we had gone through when we were arrested and taken to police stations after marches. Our fingerprints and photos were taken before we were eventually given electronic access cards. Lunch was served at the dining facility in the old wing of the parliamentary complex. To my surprise, some of the 'Whites Only / Slegs Blankes' signs had still not been removed from the toilets around the buildings. I also overheard some of the newly elected female MPs complaining that there weren't enough toilets for women, and that they had to walk past a number of men's toilets first. Up to that point the South African Parliament had never had so many female MPs.

It was rather overwhelming not just for us but also for the parliamentary staff. The African and coloured staff members, who were mainly cleaners, clerks and other administrative staff, had never served black MPs and had also never seen such a large number of female MPs. Many of them were also overcome by the fact that they were brushing shoulders with struggle stalwarts such as Mandela, Steve Tshwete and others whom they had only previously seen on TV and in newspapers.

And still we continued to make a noise, subjecting them to our struggle songs to announce our arrival in Parliament. I guess with our singing we also wanted any apartheid ghosts that might still have been hiding in those dark corridors to run for their lives.

We held our first ANC caucus meeting, a brief orientation and briefing session, in the original chamber of the National Assembly. At around 3 pm, we got into buses and were taken to the various parliamentary villages. I was among those who were allocated a house at Acacia Park, on the outskirts of Goodwood.

Acacia Park was not what I expected it to be. It consisted of a number of cheap prefabricated houses built on concrete slabs. When I opened the door to my three-bedroom house, my jaw dropped to the ground. The furniture was very old and looked like it had been taken from a museum. There was no cutlery and no linen. No one had told us we had to bring our own stuff. I stepped outside and found a few other MPs standing outside their houses in equal shock.

Apart from a small tuck shop, Acacia Park had no shops. The nearest shop was about three kilometres away, but none of us had cars. We decided to walk there so we could at least buy something to eat. Needless to say, the shop did not sell items like blankets, but even if they had, none of us had enough money to buy such things.

I owned one of the early Nokia cellphones (those that could double as a brick for protection) and so I called my wife as soon as I had settled down. I tried my best not to give her too much cause for concern about the state of our accommodation, as we had already agreed to sell our house in Kempton Park and relocate to Cape Town.

We spent the next few days in Parliament taking the oath and being sworn in as MPs. With 400 of us to be sworn in, in groups of four, the swearing-in ceremony took for ever. Still, that didn't dampen our excitement about Mandela's inauguration as the first democratically elected president of the Republic of South Africa, which took place on 10 May 1994.

My father bought me two brand-new suits, one for the inauguration and another for the official opening of Parliament on 24 May 1994. As MPs, we were given VIP tickets to the inauguration event at the Union Buildings. It was a very hot sunny day in Pretoria and the whole country was in a celebratory mood. No less than 50 heads of state attended the event, which was broadcast around the world.

With Phindi, attending President Nelson Mandela's inauguration ceremony at the Union Buildings in 1994.

The country stood still for the better part of the day, as everyone wanted to see the formal assumption of power by the black majority, the end of white minority rule and, most importantly, the final act of the liberation of the African continent.

I had come a long way from a wet-behind-the-ears protestor in Soweto in 1976. That is why I felt like pinching myself for most of that day. It almost felt unreal.

As ANC MPs we understood that the most difficult challenges – ending poverty, inequality and oppression – lay ahead. I looked forward to being part of that process. As one of the younger MPs I became what is called a backbencher, or junior member of the National Assembly. I was selected to serve on the education portfolio committee and a few other committees.

Being a backbencher involves attending committee meetings and sittings of Parliament, and participating in debates in the National Assembly. However, as a backbencher you are allocated the least amount of time to speak and yet expected to attend parliamentary sessions most of the time. (Parties are allocated speaking times based on the number of seats they have in the National Assembly, and each party decides the amount of time they allocate to their members in a debate. Party hierarchy dictates that more time is allocated to senior members such as ministers, deputy ministers, party whips and chairpersons of portfolio committees.)

It was not unheard of for a backbencher to be allocated only three minutes to speak on an important debate, such as on land reform or, in my case, the education crisis. This was the core of my disaffection with Parliament. I used to spend many hours in the parliamentary library doing research on a topic but then I would only get five minutes at the podium. I also found myself sitting in the National Assembly for hours on end listening to debates emanating from portfolio committees I wasn't part of. This was extremely frustrating and I began to doubt whether this was the best use of my time, experience and skills.

One of the primary tasks of the first democratic Parliament was to draft a new constitution, because Codesa had only produced an interim constitution. This was the only part of my stay in Parliament that I truly enjoyed, largely because of the quality of debates on important constitutional matters. During this time I read several books and articles on constitutionalism, democracy and how ordinary citizens can participate in democratic processes. I also enjoyed witnessing great minds, such as Pallo Jordan, Joe Slovo, Max Sisulu, Trevor Manuel and others, articulating their views on the Constitution and the Bill of Rights, outclassing and outsmarting the National Party MPs, who were novices on complex questions about constitutional democracy.

And then there was Madiba, who inspired me in so many ways. First, he provided strong leadership in terms of change management by assembling a diverse Cabinet that brought former enemies together. Although the individuals who served in his Cabinet came from various political parties, Madiba managed to get them all to work together for the good of the nation. Second, he inspired all South Africans to have hope and see themselves as part of the emerging 'rainbow nation'. His leadership in this regard was unprecedented and made me feel proud to be a South African. Third, he demonstrated a deep commitment to improving the conditions of the impoverished and marginalised majority by launching and overseeing the implementation of the Reconstruction and Development Programme (RDP), whose objectives were to prioritise the provision of health, education, employment and housing to the black majority. Fourth, Madiba surrounded himself with highly ethical and capable people who were usually younger and often smarter than him in certain respects. Fifth, one the most important leadership lessons he bequeathed to us was to do succession planning.

Madiba was open about the fact that he was only a ceremonial head of state, and that the person who was effectively running the country was Thabo Mbeki, who was one of the two deputy presidents at the time. Sadly, many organisations in both the public and private sectors fail to identify and prepare successors for key leadership positions, which often leaves a leadership vacuum when a popular and strong leader departs. To this day, many leadership positions in the public sector remain vacant, in some cases for years.

Finally, and probably most importantly, Madiba taught us that leaders should not overstay their welcome in leadership positions. Given his popularity in South Africa and abroad, he could easily have served a second term as president, but he only served one. This is particularly significant in the African context, where many heads of state see themselves as leaders for life.

Madiba's leadership inspired me be of service to the nation. So after a year as an MP I decided that rather than sitting in Parliament, I could be of more service to the people of South Africa as a civil servant. At that time, all levels of government were looking to appoint department heads. I had my eye on the position of superintendent-general in the Gauteng Department of Education.

During the 1994 December holidays, when I was back home in Gauteng, I started having serious discussions with comrades in the ANC structures and told them about my frustrations. My comrades and I agreed that I should apply for the position. One of the people I spoke to was Tokyo Sexwale, then Gauteng premier and the chairperson of the ANC. He undertook to speak to the national leadership but said that I should speak to the ANC leaders in Parliament.

When I didn't manage to secure a meeting with Mandela, I tried to arrange one with Mbeki. I had a tough time doing so until one day I cornered him during a session in Parliament. He had just sat down in his chair when I approached him.

'What is it then, Chief?' he said, a stern look on his face. I told him about my intention to leave Parliament.

'Chief, why don't you make an appointment with my office and we can discuss this later.'

'I've tried to make an appointment with your office before,' I said meekly.

'Try again, Chief, okay?'

Despite my best efforts, I never got that meeting, but then I was told to speak to Cyril Ramaphosa, at the time chairperson of the ANC parliamentary caucus. While he did not agree with my idea of leaving Parliament, Ramaphosa gave me permission to resign my seat. Our conversation must have lasted about 20 minutes or so, and I left feeling pleased that I had spoken to someone who had not only listened to me but also cared about what I told him.

Shortly afterwards, I heard that I had got the job as the superinten-dent-general of the Gauteng Department of Education. My long career as a civil servant was about to begin.

5

Of political heads and an early form of state capture

MY APPOINTMENT TO the Gauteng Department of Education in early 1995 meant, among other things, that I had come full circle, from being a victim of the toxic Bantu Education system to being a top civil servant tasked with ensuring equal education for all. There was a mixed response in the media to my appointment, leaning slightly to the negative side, largely because of my lack of experience in running a government department and my age (I was 31 at the time). However, I tried not to be too influenced by the criticism, as this was par for the course for newly appointed civil servants from the former liberation movements. Yes, we didn't have any experience of running a state bureaucracy, but whose fault was that, I had to ask.

Still, there were times when I felt a little overwhelmed, but I decided that I was not going to allow my lack of experience or my age get in the way. I had the courage, determination and energy to give the job my very best, and I resolved to surround myself with the best people I could find inside and outside the system.

My very first meeting was with my new boss, Mary Metcalfe, the Gauteng Member of the Executive Council (MEC) for education. I had known and worked with Metcalfe at the NECC and we were close comrades and friends. She was a highly respected educationist – hard-working and energetic – and a militant anti-apartheid activist with bright and progressive ideas on how the education system should be transformed. She was a regular presenter at the many education workshops we held with teachers, students and activists.

Metcalfe was both the best and the worst boss any civil servant could wish for. She was a workaholic who never went home until she was satisfied that every task for the day had been completed. She liked to convene early-morning meetings and would not hesitate to summon me or any official to a meeting either at her house or in the office as late as 7 pm. Metcalfe was a good leader who gave us guidance, and she never held back when she thought I or any of my officials had messed up.

She also challenged the many school governing bodies that were resisting the transformation process. For example, Metcalfe spent thousands of hours pushing former white schools to start admitting black learners. Many of the governing bodies were more open to listening to her than to me and my officials. Teachers, principals, parents, journalists and even students had her mobile number and they could call her any time. It was not uncommon for her to know about problems at a particular school before I or any of my officials did. There were times, though, when I felt that some of these constituencies used their access to her to undermine the departmental system. As officials, we often had to play catch-up, as she was always a step ahead and apparently read every single letter that was written to her. Nevertheless, Metcalfe and I had a common vision of what needed to be done, we both worked hard and we provided strong and clear leadership to our team of officials, and to principals, teachers, parents and students.

Our primary task as the leadership of the new Gauteng Department of Education was to integrate the four racially based education departments into a single, unified and non-racial system that could provide quality education for all the children in the province. By 1994 South Africa had a total of 14 education departments – ten homeland departments for Africans, one national department for Africans in the urban areas and separate departments for whites, coloureds and Indians. Each had its own curriculum, schools and pay grades for teachers and staff, and, most importantly, its own teacher training colleges. In short, we inherited a gemors (mess).

One of the first meetings the MEC and I convened was with the heads of the four education departments, all of them male. At first the meeting was quite tense, and I can only assume the four heads must have been shocked to realise that they would henceforth report to an inexperienced African activist at least 30 years their junior. I had no idea how much cooperation or resistance I would get from them. Fortunately, Metcalfe created a calm and friendly atmosphere during the meeting. She outlined our plans for integrating the department but also made sure they understood that I was now in charge.

Visiting the Germiston district as the superintendent-general of the Gauteng Department of Education with Thandi Chaane, deputy director-general.

Managing a diverse team made up of mainly men from different race groups, cultures and religions was a challenge that kept me awake at night. However, I fell back on my observations of Madiba's leadership style and drew inspiration from his vision for the country and how he used diversity to unite people.

While Madiba was a constant role model, the only direct contact I had with him during my time at the Gauteng Department of Education was when he would call to inform me that this or that business-person wanted to build a school in Gauteng and to request that I provide whatever assistance was needed to make the donation a reality. Very few of these offers materialised, but one that did was from Oprah Winfrey. My team facilitated the process to have a school built, and the Oprah Winfrey Leadership Academy for Girls opened its doors in 2007 (by which time I had left the department) and admitted more than 300 girls from disadvantaged communities.

Trying to unify the different education departments was similar to a mechanic trying to replace the engine of a bus while the bus was still in motion. We couldn't close the schools and wait until the new system was in place. The white schools were well resourced, with highly quali-fied teachers and laboratories, libraries and sports fields that could compete with the best in the world. On the other side of the system were the African, Indian and coloured schools, which had under-qualified teachers, overcrowded classrooms, a shortage of textbooks and teacher support materials, no laboratories or libraries and often not even working toilets. In many instances, prisons had better sports facilities than did township schools.

The budget allocation from National Treasury was insufficient to address the needs of the African, Indian and coloured schools, as more than 80 per cent of our budget was gobbled up by salaries, largely due to the high salaries paid to white teachers and the large number of administrators in the four departments. At the time, national govern-ment was implementing the Growth, Employment and Redistribution policy, known as GEAR, which called for a reduction in personnel expenditure. Consequently, the only way we could begin to address the needs of the black schools was by reducing our personnel costs. This was done by cutting the number of teachers and increasing class sizes in the white schools. This led to a dispute with the unions and a subsequent strike by teachers. It was a particularly difficult period for me, because for the first time I, the former activist, was on the receiving end of a strike action.

Another of our key objectives was the devolution of decision-making to district offices, which were closer to the schools and principals. We also pushed for the establishment of democratically elected school governing bodies and devolved some of the decision-making to these bodies, for instance by giving parents a say in the appointment of teachers and in admissions. Although such powers were a given in the former white schools, in African, Indian and coloured schools power had long been centralised.

Although this move helped to bridge the gap between parents and schools, it also had a number of drawbacks. For example, the governing bodies in the white schools used their additional powers to limit black children's access to 'their' schools, and the teacher unions abused their influence in governing bodies to control the teacher recruitment process.

The process of integrating the education system was progressing extremely well, and we were confident that our plan to deliver quality education to all our learners was on track. Of course, it wasn't smooth sailing all the way. We continued to face challenges around the shortage and late delivery of textbooks and learner support materials. We had decided to continue with the policy of providing free textbooks and other support materials to poor schools, as part of government's commitment to providing free primary education.

Although we were working hard to address the concerns of teachers, discipline among teachers in the townships posed a particular problem. Impromptu strikes, absenteeism and rejection of teacher assessment methods were major sources of stress for me and my team. Furthermore, integrating the IT system we used to collate matric results data and produce accurate results proved to be a bigger challenge than we anticipated. But the single and most critical challenge I faced during my time as head of the Gauteng Department of Education was the theft of matric examination papers in 1997. It threatened the credibility of the entire examination process and put the future of hundreds of students at risk.

One morning, around 1.30 am, I received a phone call from a journalist of an Afrikaans-language newspaper. She wanted to confirm reports that a mathematics exam paper that would be written later that morning had been circulated to students the previous evening. I almost fell out of my bed.

I obviously couldn't confirm or deny the story as I was unaware of the theft, but there was a strong likelihood it was true, as the journalist told me she had a copy of the examination paper in her possession. I immediately contacted my team members and the MEC and started preparing for what I knew was going to be a terrible day. We convened a crisis meeting early in the morning and decided to postpone the examination after we confirmed that the paper had indeed been leaked.

An urgent circular was sent to all the examination centres and district directors. The MEC held a media conference to inform the public about the crisis and the steps that we had taken. Fortunately, we had a back-up paper and the exam was written at a later date.

This was a major knock for the integrity of the system but we immediately took responsibility for what had happened. My team also arranged a roadshow to meet with high school principals to apologise and assure them that we were doing everything humanly possible to prevent another leak in the future.

Another important development in education in the 1990s was the introduction of outcomes-based education (OBE) by the national Department of Education. It was believed that OBE was the model most likely to address the issue of quality (and inequality) in South African education. In contrast to content-based education, OBE focuses on the outcomes of the education process; it organises the entire educational system towards what is considered essential for the learners to be able to do successfully at the end of their learning experiences.

My team and I were not convinced that the education system was ready for OBE. We believed that the change was too drastic and we did not have the time and resources to prepare the system properly. Our major concern was that the majority of the teachers, especially in the disadvantaged schools, would not be ready to embark on 360-degree system change in such a short space of time.

I appointed Enver Motala, the department's deputy director-general and an accomplished curriculum specialist, to help develop alternative proposals and to participate in the deliberations around OBE with the national department. We made our views known in all national meetings that we thought the system wasn't ready for such a radical change. Unfortunately, we were overruled and the OBE system was introduced in all schools.

Judging by what subsequently happened to the education system, especially in the township schools, I believe that the decline in the quality of education can at least partially be attributed to the fact that we rushed to implement the OBE system without taking into account the realities on the ground. Maybe we should have been more forthright in our opposition to OBE, and our failure to do so means that my team and I cannot exonerate ourselves from the challenges the education system is experiencing today.

During my time at the Gauteng Department of Education, I decided that I wanted to improve my skill set and enrolled for a Master's in

Business Administration (MBA) degree. I still don't know how I thought I would cope with my time-consuming day job and study at the same time. From a personal point of view, I later regretted my decision to do an MBA as it stole a lot of my family time. However, it did stand me in good stead when, a few years later, I became a director-general in a number of national departments.

In my last year or two as superintendent-general, my working relationship with Mary Metcalfe started to deteriorate. Increasingly, we disagreed on a number of issues. Mary held strong views on all matters relating to education in the province. She wanted to be the final decision-maker on everything, including administrative matters such as school admissions and the resolution of disputes between principals and parents, parents and teachers, etc. This encouraged schools to liaise directly with her office, and led to some schools bypassing and undermining officials on the ground. There were also reports of her having run-ins with some of my officials and meeting departmental officials without my knowledge.

I firmly believed that, unless there was a crisis at a particular school, the MEC should not be involved in administrative matters. We had an army of officials who were employed to manage schools. My primary concern was that, as the accounting officer, I had to account for everything that happened in the department and therefore could not be sidelined, especially on matters that had budgetary implications. I was of the view that if she had concerns about the performance of officials, including me, these should be brought to my attention so that I could take action. Sadly, some of these disputes ended up with Mary asking the Gauteng Public Service Commission to investigate certain officials for insubordination. This created tensions in the department, as officials and staff felt torn between their support for me and support for the MEC.

At the heart of my conflict with Mary Metcalfe was something I later learnt was called the political-administrative interface. A successful political-administrative interface in the public service requires clearly defined roles for politicians on the one hand and civil servants on the other. According to Janet Kathyola, a Malawian public-sector management advisor, good governance requires the separation of political functions from administrative ones, while at the same time ensuring a clear point of connection between the two, since both functions are mutually reinforcing. When there is political interference in the work done by civil servants, these functions become blurred.[8]

Challenges around the political-administrative interface remain an issue in the public service to this day. To my mind, the lack of clarity around the respective roles of politicians and senior public servants, and the conflict this creates, is one of the major contributing factors to the brain drain in the public service. It is also a contributing factor in the reported tension between the boards and CEOs of state-owned enterprises (SOEs) on the one hand and the shareholder ministers on the other.

The democratic government's apparent inability to find a lasting solution to this matter should be of great concern to all South Africans, as it poses a serious risk to the public sector's ability to attract and retain professionals of all races. The public service should be normalised and professionalised as a matter of urgency to attract urgently needed skills. We could also learn from established democracies that seem to have found workable models in this regard.

Before my conflict with Metcalfe could spiral out of control, my term as superintendent-general came to an end. I felt my team at the education department had laid a solid foundation to take education in Gauteng to the next level. The time had come for me to move on.

After I left the civil service in 2000, a short stint in the private sector followed. I joined the Damelin Education Group as managing director but soon discovered that the holding company was being sold to Naspers by its founders and that Damelin was in need of a capital injection. The new owners were unhappy about the company's per-formance but were not willing to spend much money and started put-ting what I felt was undue pressure on me and my management team. Five months after I started the job, I left the company.

For about a year and a half I didn't have full-time employment and dabbled in different things. Towards the end of 2002 a number of director-general positions in various national departments were being advertised, including for the Department of Public Works. I thought it could be an interesting challenge – I have always had an interest in the role public works could play in job creation – and so I applied. In January 2003, I was informed by letter that I had got the job. I was thrilled finally to be part of national government. My political head would be Stella Sigcau, a Xhosa princess who had been, briefly, the first female prime minister of the Transkei homeland before she was deposed by Brigadier Bantu Holomisa in 1987. Interestingly, in Sep-tember 1996 Holomisa was fired from Cabinet by President Mbeki after publicly accusing Sigcau of accepting a R50 000 bribe from Chief George Matanzima, the former ruler of the Transkei homeland. Holomisa went on to form the United Democratic Movement (UDM) after his dismissal from the ANC.

By the time I joined the Department of Public Works it was already suffering from leadership instability and below-average performance, partially caused by the high turnover of directors-general. This insta-bility had a major impact on staff morale, and the lack of strategic direction also led to numerous qualified audits by the Auditor-General. Thus, one of my first duties as the new director-general was to appear before Parliament's Standing Committee on Public Accounts to account for the unauthorised expenditure incurred by the department and for its failure to address the audit inquiries from previous years.

The public works department was good at spending its maintenance budget and yet the conditions of government facilities were deterio-rating. I would receive numerous calls from ministers, deputy ministers, directors-general and other heads of state institutions complaining about poor service delivery from the department. When I would summon officials to explain why we were spending billions of rands on maintenance, without any visible signs of improvement, they were very good at bullshitting their way out of the situation.

This went on for a while until I was approached by the State Information and Technology Agency (SITA), which informed me that they had procured business intelligence software to help national departments get control over their expenditure and manage project implementation. I informed the relevant officials about the software and indicated that I wanted us to participate in the project. I immediately sensed resistance from some of the sections that were responsible for the building and maintenance programme in the department. Sadly, my term ended before I could ensure that the SITA project was implemented. I suspect that some of the officials resisted the implementation of the software for fear that it would establish a monitoring system and give the department control over the expenditure of more than R1 billion on maintenance – with nothing or very little to show for it. At the time, this information was outsourced to private companies, which controlled what I considered to be departmental information.

Three incidents of what I call 'inexplicable expenditure' are worth sharing. In the first I was summoned by Zanele Mbeki, the wife of then President Thabo Mbeki, to a meeting at Genadendal, the official presidential residence in Cape Town. She took me on a tour of the house and showed me the many leaks in the roof that she had been complaining about for months without any response from the Department of Public Works. The leaks were so bad that the carpets had started to rot and were giving off a bad odour. I was embarrassed to see buckets being used to catch the water in the passages.

I apologised profusely to the First Lady and promised to address the problem immediately. I discovered that the department did not have internal capacity to fix the problem. In the end it took more than six months to procure the services of an external service provider, because the identified company still had to go through a security vetting process by the National Intelligence Agency (NIA), currently the Domestic Branch of the State Security Agency. I soon realised that one of the major causes of poor service delivery was the policy decision to outsource most of the department's functions in an attempt to reduce personnel costs.

In the second instance, Kathy Satchwell, a judge in the Johannesburg High Court, summoned me to her office to complain about the state of the courtroom where she worked. For one thing, the air conditioning was out of order. I had met Satchwell during my activist days at Wits; she had acted as our attorney when I and my fellow activists were arrested after the numerous protest marches on and off campus. Once again, I had to apologise profusely. When I demanded an explanation from the relevant officials, they gave world-class excuses about why they had not fixed the problems at the court. I instructed them to deal with the matter as soon as possible.

However, when I bumped into Kathy at a function a few months later and asked whether the problem had been fixed, she politely said that it hadn't. I was furious and embarrassed. I immediately summoned the Johannesburg regional director and instructed him to attend to the matter urgently. It was resolved within a month.

The third instance was when I was summoned by the Presidency and officials of the South African National Defence Force to join them at 1 Military Hospital in Pretoria to discuss conditions there. The hospital tends to the medical needs of military personnel, as well as to those of the president and other heads of state. I had never been there before and was expecting a top-class facility. What I found was uncut grass, half-lit and dark corridors, a few broken windows, lifts out of order and the most unwelcoming reception area imaginable. My tour of the hospital left me flabbergasted. I looked at the maintenance budget for that year and what we had spent at the facility in the previous financial years. What I saw at the hospital did not match the amount of money the department had allegedly spent there. Once again, my officials had the best of excuses.

This matter was of great concern to me, yet the officials based at head office did not seem to be concerned about the state of affairs in the department. When I looked into the contracts for their performance bonuses, I saw that their bonuses depended solely on whether they spent their budgets and not on whether they achieved the required outcomes.

The department's budget was made up of 'own budget' allocation from National Treasury and funds we received from sister departments to maintain their facilities. I was concerned about where the money was going and decided to dig deeper to understand what was going on. I gathered data about the building and maintenance section of the department, focusing on expenditure trends, management processes, procurement procedures and the personnel who were involved. I discovered that a large part of the department's function was outsourced, including project management, budgeting and procurement. External companies were performing most of these functions to a point where all management reports were generated externally. If I called for a report on a particular project such as 1 Military Hospital, my staff would call the external company to produce the report. This meant that an external company was controlling all our data and was integral to the procurement process, including identifying projects, preparing tender specifications, preparing tender adverts, shortlisting potential bidders and recommending successful bidders.

I continued to dig and found that a handful of white-owned companies were winning tenders on a regular basis, to the exclusion of many small and emerging black and white companies. Not only was this a matter of dubious procurement principles but it also posed a security risk, as these companies had access to and controlled sensitive procurement information, for instance about key points such as military facilities. Worst of all, they were being paid billions to maintain state facilities without there being any visible improvement. Clearly taxpayers' money was being wasted.

I reported the matter to Stella Sigcau and she agreed that the matter should be reported to the National Prosecuting Authority (NPA) and the Directorate of Special Operations, or Scorpions (a multidisciplinary agency that investigated organised crime and corruption before it was disbanded in 2009).

During my investigation I compiled several lever arch files, which I then handed over to Vusi Pikoli, the head of the NPA at the time. In addition, I tried to restructure the department and introduced the position of chief operations officer to help manage and streamline operations, but the problems continued unabated.

Soon, a number of departments started to demand that the maintenance function should be returned to them. The Department of Trade and Industry was the first department to declare a UDI (unilateral declaration of independence) and procure its own building, after the Department of Public Works failed to deliver.

Despite the many challenges, there were also successes. One of the projects I had to take over and help drive when I joined the department in February 2003 was the Expanded Public Works Programme (EPWP). This programme was meant to address the unemployment crisis, and a target was set of creating one million job opportunities by 2009.

The Cabinet's economic cluster was given the mandate to develop the programme, and public works became the lead department in this regard. Stella Sigcau had presented a draft programme to the Cabinet lekgotla in January 2003, but this had been rejected for lacking details. I put together an interdepartmental task team that developed a revised proposal, which was presented to Cabinet in March.

During this meeting, President Mbeki didn't participate in the initial discussion, as he was supposed to give the closing remarks. When it was his turn to speak, he gave an extensive critique of the proposal, which amounted to a rejection of what we had presented. He basically sent us packing.

Mbeki was able to pick up inconsistencies and inaccuracies in our presentation that were not supported or by data that contradicted the various reports we had included in the files. He had not only read the presentation but had also read the five or six supporting documents and research reports we had submitted to all the ministers in advance. To say we were caught off-guard and just a little humiliated is an understatement!

I managed to steal a moment with Mbeki during the break and requested a meeting to discuss his thoughts on how we could strengthen the proposal. His staff called to schedule a meeting for that Sunday afternoon at his office in the Union Buildings. I wasted no time in getting a task team together and we worked around the clock to address Mbeki's concerns. Mfezeko Gwazube, a bright young University of Cape Town engineering graduate who had been seconded to my office, helped me to complete our proposal by that Saturday evening.

Mfezeko and I drove to the Union Buildings and arrived about an hour before the scheduled time, as Mbeki was known to be a stickler for punctuality. I was quite nervous and anxious. When his secretary ushered us into the office, Mbeki was sitting behind his desk reading something. He invited us to take a seat and shortly afterwards we started the presentation. I introduced the strategic framework of the proposal and Mfezeko presented the technical aspects and the numbers, including the job opportunities it would create.

Mbeki listened attentively. When we were finished, he went to fetch his pipe from his desk and kept quiet for a very long time. Then he looked at me and said, 'Well done, Chief . . . this mutter [he always pronounced "matter" like this] is a very important intervention and we need to make sure that we get it right and ensure that all spheres of government are involved in the implementation process.' He said something to the effect that he was pleased that we had read this and that report on unemployment and job creation in other countries. He stood up and shook our hands, and we wasted no time in leaving his office in case he changed his mind and give us additional work. The meeting took about 45 minutes – 42 of which were taken up by our presentation.

The EPWP proposal was presented at the next Cabinet meeting and became one of the key programmes announced by Mbeki in his State of the Nation Address that year. The EPWP programme became one of government's flagship initiatives and created thousands of job opportunities around the country.

Those who criticise public works programmes in general, and the EPWP in particular, for not creating permanent and well-paying jobs miss the point that these programmes are neither designed nor intended to resolve the unemployment problem. They seek to address the effects of unemployment, particularly poverty. They try to put food on the table and provide the poor with basic skills.

In my second year in the department, my relationship with Stella Sigcau became increasingly strained. At the start of my tenure we would have weekly meetings in her office. Initially, these meetings were productive and I used them to update her about key projects. However, as our relationship deteriorated, they became a nightmare. The minister used the meetings to stamp her authority and give instructions that were not always the most prudent or, worst of all, were procedurally incorrect.

I tried hard to avoid any disagreement with the minister in front of my officials, but they soon picked up on the tension between us. Some of them abused the situation to push projects and activities they knew I would not approve of. The situation became untenable when certain officials got approvals for projects directly from the minister and expected me to simply sign off on them and authorise the expenditure. The more I declined such projects, the frostier the relationship with the minister became.

By 2005, the third year of my contract, I became very unhappy with my working conditions. I sought advice from a number of directors-general and to my surprise realised that I wasn't the only person who had these kinds of problems with my political head. Fortunately, Cabinet had approved an amendment to the Public Service Act stipulating that directors-general were appointed by the president and not by ministers. This ensured that a minister could no longer get rid of a director-general at will.

On a related note, in the first few years after the 1994 democratic elections, directors-general were employed on five-year contracts. However, government became concerned when directors-general started leaving their positions ahead of the end of their contracts due to conflicts with their ministers. This came at great cost to the taxpayer because government was obliged to pay the remainder of the director-general's term. Cabinet then decided to reduce the contract period to three years.

The unintended consequence of this move was a brain drain of highly experienced individuals from the civil service. In addition, it made these positions less attractive to external candidates, since few people would want to leave a permanent job in the private sector to take a job with a three-year term. This matter was debated extensively at the Forum of South African Directors-General (Fosad) and there was consensus that reducing the contract period was not the solution to the problem of conflict between ministers and their directors-general.

I sought an audience with Mbeki to seek his intervention. He undertook to look into the matter and meet with the minister as soon as possible, but I never heard back from him. I suspect Sigcau somehow got to know of my meeting with Mbeki, since our relationship deteriorated even further. She cancelled all our weekly meetings and declined all my requests for meetings.

The next thing, I received a hand-delivered letter informing me that my contract would not be extended. I felt I had made a positive contribution towards fixing the many operational challenges the department was experiencing. For one, in my second year in the department, my team and I had achieved a significant milestone when we tabled one of the very rare unqualified audit reports to Parliament. I was sad and disappointed, as I thought I deserved a more dignified departure.

Unfortunately, by the time I left, there had been no feedback from Vusi Pikoli about my investigation into public works department tenders being awarded to white-owned companies. Now there would be no opportunity to follow up on the matter.

However, after three gruelling years in the department I was looking forward to having more time for myself and my family, as the job had turned me into an absent father. I had missed out on so many of my sons' sports activities and parents' meetings. I also needed more time to think about my next career move. Joining the private sector was uppermost in my mind.

6

I become government spokesperson

ONE DAY IN the first half of 2006, I was out on the golf course when I received a call from Joel Netshitenzhe, then CEO of the Government Communication and Information System (GCIS) and government spokesperson. As Joel was not known for making social calls, I immediately knew something was up. He soon came to the reason for his call, and told me I should consider returning to government.

'Joel, have you been smoking something?' I said and burst out laughing.

I had known Joel since my days in the struggle and had had several interactions with him at Fosad level during my stint as director-general of public works. He was also one of the directors-general I had confided in about my difficulties with Stella Sigcau. He was one of only a handful of people who knew I had even discussed my problems with President Thabo Mbeki.

Joel spent the next few minutes explaining why he thought it was important for me to return to government. I know very few people who could say no to Joel when he asked something of them and I think he was aware of this.

'Which department do you have in mind?' I asked.

'Come see me, then I'll tell you,' he said.

A few days later, I went to see him at his office in the Union Buildings. He told me that the position of CEO of GCIS would be available soon as he was going to be leading the Policy Coordination and Advisory Services (PCAS) unit in Mbeki's office. The PCAS was responsible for ensuring proper policy coordination within government. (Eventually, most if not all policy initiatives in government went through Joel and his team before being approved by Cabinet.)

Joel thought I would be a good replacement for him.

'Joel, as you know, I have never even worked in communications and I don't have any formal training in the field. I know dangerously little about communications,' I said.

He didn't seem even a little perturbed by my response.

'Of course, I'm not in a position to offer the position to you, but I'm willing to put your name forward. And remember, I will only be a phone call away if you get the job.'

I said I would seriously consider it and get back to him in a few days. As I walked out, he told me to update my CV and be ready to submit my application as soon as the GCIS position was advertised. Clearly, he would not take no for an answer. After discussing the matter with my family, I decided to go ahead and apply.

I was shortlisted and invited to attend interviews at the Union Buildings, where I was grilled for at least an hour by the interview panel, which consisted of Joel and Essop Pahad, the minister in the Presidency responsible for government communications, and two other ministers. I was elated when I heard a few weeks later that Cabinet had approved my appointment. I couldn't believe I'd got it.

Before starting my new job, I read numerous books, journals and articles on government communications. As I had previously participated in the Senior Executive Programme, an intensive six-week management course jointly offered by Wits University and the John F

Kennedy School of Government at Harvard University, I had access to the Harvard education portal, where I found numerous articles on government communication departments in other parts of the world. Of course, I also studied GCIS documents, reports and presentations to Parliament.

One of my first meetings as CEO of GCIS was a briefing session with Joel and Essop Pahad, who would be my new boss. The two briefed me about my responsibilities at GCIS and also informed me that I had to attend all Cabinet meetings and announce Cabinet decisions. I froze when I heard this because I wasn't aware it was part of the job. I was both excited and anxious about this aspect of my work. It didn't take me long to realise that being CEO of GCIS and being the spokesperson for the government or Cabinet were two very distinct jobs, each with its own unique specifications and challenges.

After meeting senior members of my department, I was confident that I would make it in the job. I realised that I was surrounded by

At a GCIS Government Communicators Awards ceremony
with Joel Netshitenzhe (middle) and Minister Richard Baloyi (right).

extremely capable colleagues who were energetic, experienced, hard-working and, most importantly, proud to be working at GCIS. I was also impressed by the management processes and systems that I found in the department.

One of the things I had come to dislike intensely was the length of meetings in government departments. When I arrived for my first GCIS management meeting, I was told that the lady who prepared breakfast was running late. I was surprised, as I assumed that, like me, everyone had their breakfast at home. After the lady got there and served breakfast, she started taking orders for lunch and asked if she would be required to prepare dinner too. I was confused.

Then I was told that the management meeting usually took up the whole day and often only finished in the early evening. I wasted no time in telling my team that, going forward, there would be no more day-long meetings and food would no longer be served. I told them that we should all have breakfast at home and that meetings must be concluded by lunch time.

I established that the reasons for the length of these meetings were that documents were only circulated at the meeting, there were many long presentations and everyone wanted to speak. External people were also invited to make presentations. I told the team that documents and presentations had to be circulated a day or two in advance and then be taken as read when the meeting took place. Team members had to summarise their presentations, and I also instructed the team that external presentations should be given at divisional meetings and would only be made at the management level in exceptional cases. Thereafter we held shorter and more productive meetings and still had the rest of the day to undertake other duties.

As CEO of the department, I had to manage the operations of the department, review and implement its strategic plan, provide overall strategic direction and have oversight of its budget, monitor performance, ensure proper coordination with heads of communication from sister departments and report to the minister and to Parliament.

One of my main tasks was to develop key messages on behalf of the entire government. We commissioned research on various topical issues and regular perception surveys so that we knew at any given time what citizens were concerned about, what information was needed by communities and stakeholders and what they thought about government and the performance of leaders, including the president. We wanted to ensure that government messages addressed the needs of society and that our work should not be mere propaganda.

Our messages were communicated through print, electronic media and direct engagement with communities through what we called the Izimbizo programme. This also involved setting up community meetings where the president and his ministers could meet communities directly to inform them of what government was doing and to listen to what their expectations were of government. We were very clear that government communication was not only about broadcasting messages but also about listening to the voters.

The Izimbizo programme was intensive and required a lot of planning and coordination between GCIS, the Presidency and the offices of the provincial premiers. We were always amazed by the attendance figures at these gatherings – clearly, citizens always welcomed the opportunity to spend a day with their public representatives. Sadly, this programme was discontinued when Jacob Zuma became president in May 2009.

Our stakeholder engagement programme included social gatherings with journalists, which were often hosted and sponsored by the different media houses. One of our strategic objectives was to build a strong relationship with the media.

Another aspect of stakeholder engagement was what we called 'development communication', which was about getting government closer to citizens. The two-part programme entailed employing com

*At a meeting between members of the South African National Editors Forum,
President Thabo Mbeki and other government representatives in Pretoria.*
(Credit: Arena Holdings)

munication officers in townships and villages around the country
and promoting the establishment of service centres in communities.
We helped to open many multipurpose community centres where
different government departments opened branches in these communities. Our communication officers worked closely with development officers to identify families who qualified for social grants and
helped them to apply for and access these.

As CEO of GCIS I was also automatically a board member of the
International Marketing Council (IMC, today known as Brand South
Africa). This agency was established to assist government to manage
the country brand and to market South Africa to the rest of the world.
GCIS was, and still is, responsible for the overall management of the
country brand. The agency's board was made up of CEOs of private
companies and other business leaders, the directors-general of the
departments of Tourism and Foreign Affairs and the CEO of GCIS.

If I had to rate the briefing I received from Joel Netshitenzhe and Essop Pahad, in terms of making sure I knew exactly what my new job would entail, I would have to give them a four out of ten. For instance, they made the job of being government spokesperson sound so easy – 'Simply attend Cabinet meetings and issue a statement afterwards,' they'd said. Little did I know that this part of my job would consume more time than any other position I've ever held in my life.

Small details they left out included the amount of reading I would need to do before each Cabinet meeting, the impact of travelling to Cape Town on a weekly basis, having to keep my phone on 24 hours a day, doing radio and TV interviews, and arguing with ministers who spoke out of turn or said something I considered damaging to the reputation of government. I had to find my way around all of these issues, and unfortunately Joel was not always there to hold my hand.

My team at GCIS did their best to support me, but since I was the only one who was allowed to attend Cabinet meetings, there was a limit to what they could do. My job involved more than just communicating Cabinet decisions, which is why I was the government spokesperson instead of just the Cabinet spokesperson. I could speak on behalf of government even when Cabinet was not in session because some communication issues could not wait for a Cabinet meeting before government issued a response, and some issues did not necessarily need Cabinet discussion for government's voice to be heard.

My first Cabinet meeting was at the Union Buildings, and since Pahad had warned me to be punctual I made sure I was seated by the time everyone arrived. When I got to my seat, the secretariat handed me four lever arch files and told me they contained the documents pertaining to that day's meeting. Pahad introduced me to Cabinet just before the meeting started. Needless to say, my palms were a bit sweaty and I felt tense.

I took detailed notes of the discussions, but what made my task easier that day was that Mbeki, who did not participate actively in most of the discussions, came in at the end to summarise the key issues and state what the decision on a specific matter should be. This is not going to be that difficult, I thought. All I needed to do was to wait for the president's summary at the end of each meeting and turn that into my statement.

Apart from conveying the key decision, I also had to explain the background to each decision, the rationale behind it, as well as its implications. All that information would be found in those lever arch files. To make things worse, at that time the press briefing was always held on the same day as the Cabinet meeting. Again, it was a small detail that Joel and Essop hadn't told me about.

My first media conference was quite a disaster. I was unprepared and the journalists didn't do me any favours, asking questions as if I had been doing the job for the past 20 years. My standard response that day was, 'I will get back to you on that one.'

I immediately made the call to change the time of the media briefing to 10 am the day after the Cabinet meeting. Having it on the same

*At a post-Cabinet media briefing with Rob Davies (right),
then minister of the Department of Trade and Industry.*

day not only put too much pressure on me and my team but also opened us up to mistakes. If the briefing was the next morning, it also gave me the whole day to conduct radio and television interviews.

Cabinet meeting weeks always kicked off with me and my team either receiving or chasing the Cabinet file. Once the file was received, we would spend most of the day studying it and identifying all the key communication issues for the media statements to be issued after the Cabinet meeting. The Tuesday before the Cabinet meeting involved drafting what we called the 'current affairs' document that would be submitted to Cabinet the following morning.

My team would conduct a quick survey of major events and news stories and identify three or four issues that we thought Cabinet should express itself on. This document was typically finalised on the morning of the Cabinet meeting, and it was the only document that was distributed at the meeting and not circulated two weeks beforehand.

After the meeting, my team and I would often still be exchanging emails and calls until the early hours of the morning. There were times when I would wake up and not remember which draft I should be working on. On good days, I would have a final draft on my laptop before I went to bed. But soon our system was running like clockwork.

The media conference held the day after the Cabinet meeting started sharply at 10 am, and there were a few times when I had to reprimand journalists for arriving late. I should, however, also confess that at least two of my media briefings started about 20 minutes late after the GCIS printers misbehaved and we couldn't print our statement in time.

It was hard work but it was also satisfying. The communication bug had bitten me! I understood my task to be not only about holding up a loudhailer for government and telling citizens about Cabinet decisions but also about bringing government closer to its citizens. As a government communicator, I served multiple stakeholders, including my employer (government), the media, the public and my team.

One of the exciting projects my team and I worked on was to revamp the media centres at the Union Buildings and Parliament. We turned them into state-of-the-art facilities, with a video link that allowed us to hold a media conference with journalists in Cape Town and Pretoria at the same time. Over time, I built up good working relationships with most of the journalists because I was always available to answer their calls.

I did my best to keep my mobile phone on at all times because I believed that being accessible to the media and other government communicators was an important part of a communicator's job. Looking back, I realise that I was not very successful in striking a balance between my work and my private life. There were times when I was supposed to spend quality time with my family and I was always on my phone.

My approach was also to be truthful and never be afraid to say, 'I don't know the answer to your question, but I'll come back to you.' When it comes to the media, though, one should know that 'later' should be 'as soon as possible'. My view was that government communicators and journalists should be partners who understood that they needed one another in order to be successful in their respective jobs. One of the many complaints I used to get from journalists was that some of my colleagues in the communication units of other government departments were not always accessible, especially when a response was needed on a major news story. There were times when my team and I desperately tried to track down a communicator who was nowhere to be found during a crisis involving a minister or their department.

My team and I constantly raised the issue of accessibility during our interdepartmental meetings with other communicators. I learnt that part of the problem was that some of the communicators did not have good relationships with their political principals and were scared to make mistakes or didn't want to be accused of 'miscommunicating' by their principals.

Top: *With Essop Pahad and award recipients at the Government
Communicators Awards in 2009.*
Bottom: *Addressing my team at a monthly meeting at the
GCIS head office in Pretoria.*

We were also concerned that a number of our political leaders were
not good communicators, and a few had particularly poor relationships
with the media and saw journalists as the enemy. These leaders forgot

that when they were dealing with journalists, they were in effect communicating with the public and not just the journalist in front of them. We tried many times to arrange media training sessions for ministers, but these sessions were not always well-attended due to the ministers' busy schedules. There was also a perception that such training was a waste of time.

Once Mbeki agreed that a part of one of the Cabinet meetings could be dedicated to media training, I procured the services of a media training company. Mbeki himself declined to be part of the training since he believed he knew how to deal with the media. Sadly, he and the majority of ministers did not participate in the training session. I still believe basic communication training should be part of the orientation programme when a minister assumes office.

In stark contrast to my relationship with Stella Sigcau, I established a good partnership with Essop Pahad based on mutual trust and respect. I had easy access to him and we would regularly meet to discuss the Cabinet agenda. Often, when I called him to ask whether he wanted to see the Cabinet statements before I released them, he would say, 'Hey, Chief, you were at the meeting, you don't need me to approve the statement.'

He would call me at odd hours to ask me to speak to a minister who had uttered something in the media that was contrary to government policy. Then the respective minister's statement would be withdrawn within days. Pahad never pulled any punches when it came to dealing with ministers who went against the will of the collective.

During Mbeki's tenure, I had access both to him as president and to his staff, as it was important for all of us to ensure that government messages were properly aligned. There would be times when Cabinet was dealing with complex and fairly controversial matters and many different views were expressed during a meeting. When the final decision wasn't clear to me, I would steal a few minutes of Mbeki's time directly after the meeting to check that I was conveying the correct message to the public.

In other instances, the decision might be clear but I would be concerned about the impact and timing of it. His advice in this regard was always incredibly valuable. I felt I could communicate confidently with the knowledge that I had his full support. Nothing makes a communicator more effective than clarity of thought from his or her principals, and nothing is more frustrating than a boss who cannot give direction when he or she is required to do so.

Mbeki managed his Cabinet well, and I got the sense that he enjoyed the full confidence and respect of his ministers. He was always punctual for meetings, and he rarely participated at the beginning of a discussion. When he listened to the debates, he would often stare at the ceiling with his eyes closed – but never to be mistaken for dozing off. Those who had to make presentations knew they had to be well-prepared because Mbeki always prepared for Cabinet meetings.

It was even more fascinating to watch Mbeki in action at the biannual Cabinet *makgotla* (the plural of lekgotla), which were attended by all ministers, deputy ministers, premiers and national and provincial directors-general. The primary objective of these gatherings was to review the government's programme of action and to plan for the coming year. Each of the five government clusters had to do presentations here in an effort to get the green light to implement their programmes.

The Mbeki factor made these meetings quite stressful for both ministers and their directors-general. As I'd learnt from personal experience, Mbeki would often read not only the presentations but also the supporting documents in advance. He listened attentively to the presentations and allowed everyone to ask questions and make their comments before offering his input right at the end. In many instances he also did his own research, which often caught the presenting team off-guard. The economics cluster had a particularly rough time and were always sent back to redo their presentations because Mbeki, who is very knowledgeable on the subject, would raise questions that none of the ministers or directors-general had thought of. He was truly impressive.

Whenever Mbeki was about to give a media conference, I would spend at least an hour or so with him to discuss the media statement, which would have been prepared by his communication team. Mbeki was always willing to listen to my communication advice and never hesitated to express his views when he thought the advice sounded more like PR than truly sharing information with the public.

With President Thabo Mbeki (right) on the way to a meet-and-greet with members of the parliamentary press group following the debate on his State of the Nation address.

However, he did not always heed my advice and there were times when I felt communication was not a major priority for him. For instance, when xenophobic violence broke out in Johannesburg in May 2008, I was attending a meeting of Mbeki's Presidential International Advisory Council on Information Society and Development in Pietermaritzburg. This was a forum bringing together global CEOs of information technology (IT) companies to advise government on IT strategy. I received a call from a GCIS field worker who informed me that there were reports of foreign-owned shops in City Deep,

Johannesburg, being looted, and a number of foreign nationals had been attacked.

I asked for a few minutes with Mbeki to alert him to this development. He agreed to see me during the tea break, but he seemed rather annoyed that I was briefing him about a matter that he thought he should have been briefed on by the security departments. While he was disturbed by the news, he thought it was too soon to describe it as xenophobic violence. He told me in no uncertain terms that it was a criminal matter that had to be addressed by the police, and that he didn't view it as either a communication or a xenophobic matter.

I tried to explain to him that the negative media coverage could potentially undermine his global standing, especially at a time when he was meeting with the CEOs of major IT companies. But he was unmoved, and I left feeling that I had wasted his time. In the end, 62 people died and thousands were displaced in xenophobic violence that soon spread to the rest of the country.[9] It tarnished South Africa's reputation and damaged relationships with a number of African countries whose citizens were murdered. Disappointingly, Mbeki didn't seem to appreciate the seriousness of the matter. I was deflated.

During Mbeki's tenure, the director-general in the Presidency was the Reverend Frank Chikane, a veteran anti-apartheid activist whom I knew from my days as an activist. One Sunday afternoon in September 2007, I received a call from the soft-spoken Chikane.

'Where are you, Chief, are you busy?'

I told him that I was in Johannesburg spending time with my wife.

'I'm sorry, Themba, but we need you at Mahlamba Ndlopfu [the presidential residence in Pretoria] immediately. The president needs to see you before he goes to the US to attend the United Nations General Assembly.'

Chikane didn't go into details, and my first thought was that I was in trouble. Within minutes I was in my car and on my way. When I drove into the estate, I realised I was still in shorts and a golf shirt; I was in such a rush that I hadn't thought to change into more formal clothes. It was too late, though, so I grabbed my notepad and pen and walked towards the entrance.

The next moment Vusi Pikoli, at the time the National Director of Public Prosecutions (NDPP), stepped out the front door. We shook hands but he seemed preoccupied and in a hurry. He leant in and whispered something in my ear, but I couldn't hear what he was saying. Pikoli had a reputation as a no-nonsense guy who prosecuted friend and foe alike if they broke the law. Now I was really getting worried.

A butler ushered me into the main lounge, where I was met by Mbeki, Chikane, justice minister Brigitte Mabandla and Mojanku Gumbi, the president's legal advisor. Mbeki looked rather anxious. He started to explain that they just had a very difficult meeting with Pikoli. Mbeki then told me that about two weeks earlier, on 10 September 2007, the NPA had issued a warrant of arrest for National Police Commissioner Jackie Selebi on charges of corruption, fraud, racketeering and defeating the ends of justice. Some of the charges related to Selebi's friendship with convicted drug smuggler Glenn Agliotti.

Mbeki said he was concerned about the security implications if the office of a sitting commissioner was raided and the commissioner arrested. He had asked Mabandla to persuade Pikoli to delay Selebi's arrest and the laying of formal charges, but Pikoli had refused. Mbeki emphasised that he had not asked Pikoli not to prosecute Selebi, but rather to give him two weeks to prepare as the arrest of the National Commissioner of Police would have a serious impact. Pikoli had flatly refused and insisted that the president's request amounted to interference by the executive in the judicial process.

Moreover, the president indicated that all his attempts to mediate between Mabandla and Pikoli had failed. Mabandla added that she had tried her best to have a sober conversation with Pikoli but had found him 'too stubborn' and 'intransigent'. Mbeki therefore concluded that the relationship between the justice minister and Pikoli had broken down irretrievably. Pikoli had also informed Mbeki that Selebi's arrest and prosecution was imminent, and the president interpreted this as open defiance. For all these reasons, he had decided to suspend Pikoli with immediate effect and set up an inquiry to investigate his fitness to hold office.

As the president spoke, I sank deeper and deeper into my chair while feverishly taking notes. 'So, Chief,' the President continued, 'we want you to announce this decision today.'

At the heart of the conflict between the two was Section 179 of the Constitution. Section 179 (4) stipulates that the prosecuting authority (NDPP) must exercise its functions 'without fear, favour or prejudice', while Section 179 (6) states that 'the Cabinet member responsible for the administration of justice must exercise final responsibility over the prosecuting authority'. Mabandla clearly felt Section 179 (6) gave her a say in decisions relating to prosecutions, while Pikoli believed he could prosecute without interference from the minister.

I took a deep breath and went through my notes again and again to make sure I understood what had just transpired. I had a few questions.

'Mr President, is this the decision final and were all legal prescripts followed?' I asked.

The president answered in the affirmative on both counts and then had to leave the meeting.

I tried to convince the three remaining officials to delay the announcement by a day to give me more time to plan, but they insisted that the announcement could not be delayed as the story could easily leak to the media. I knew there would be much controversy around the announcement, if only because the Constitution held that the NDPP was an independent institution.

After I left the house I sat in my car for at least 30 minutes trying to get my head around the storm that was about to break. I also thought about Pikoli, whom I had known since his days as the director-general in the Department of Justice and had great respect for. I found him a very serious guy who was not afraid to speak his mind in the many Fosad meetings we had attended together. And now I had to announce his suspension. I tried to call him on his mobile phone but couldn't reach him. I was sad for him, and I also wondered how Girly, his wife and a fellow civil servant, was going to take the news.

As I drove out of the Mahlamba Ndlopfu complex, I started calling my GCIS lieutenants and informing them that I had just been given a difficult and urgent statement to draft. I would need them to help in editing it. They sounded as shocked as I was when first told about the decision. I told them that our job was to announce and not to question the decision of our principals.

Once I was finished, I called Pahad to ensure he was aware of the decision before I sent out the statement. I read him my draft over the phone. He also wanted to know why the decision was so urgent that it had to be announced on a Sunday before Cabinet could be briefed. I answered his questions to the best of my ability. Clearly, he was also worried about the public fallout from the announcement.

I read the final draft no fewer than six times before I gave the team the go-ahead to issue the statement. It cited the 'irretrievable break-down in the working relationship' between the minister of justice and the NDPP as the primary reason for Pikoli's suspension.[10] Advocate Mokotedi Mpshe was appointed as acting National Director of Public Prosecutions. I drove home as quickly as I could because I knew I would have to start conducting interviews immediately.

The next 48 hours were hell on earth. My phone rang off the hook within minutes of the statement reaching the media. I received calls from newspapers, TV channels and radio stations I never even knew existed. It even generated interest from overseas media houses – an indication of the degree of interest from the international community in our young democracy.

The South African Broadcasting Corporation (SABC) insisted on a live interview, which I accepted on condition that they come to my house, which they did. I only slept for a few hours that Sunday night and had to be up early the next morning for live radio and TV interviews. I also got a lot of calls from ministers and directors-general who wanted to confirm the news. If there ever was a story that nearly broke my back as government spokesperson, this was it.

The pressure on me was compounded by the fact that Mbeki was on a flight to New York when the story broke and neither he nor his spokesperson could conduct any interviews. In many respects, and in a very literal sense, I became the face of the decision to suspend Pikoli, as my photo was splashed on the front pages of newspapers and on television. A few times I was stopped in the streets by people who thought I was Pikoli because my face had become synonymous with the story, others even accused me of suspending Pikoli.

Although I executed the task to the best of my ability, I wasn't entirely convinced about the correctness or the timing of the decision. Unsurprisingly, the media coverage of Pikoli's suspension was very negative and the entire affair reflected badly on Mbeki's reputation as a constitutionalist. It also reinforced the belief held by some that Mbeki had tried to protect Selebi due to their close friendship. While I was sympathetic to Mbeki's view that a fight between the top cop and the top prosecutor could undermine the security of the state, I was not convinced that suspending the NDPP for trying to do his job was the right decision.

As my team and I had anticipated, Mbeki returned to a political storm, with opposition parties crying foul. On 30 September, he appointed former parliamentary speaker Frene Ginwala to chair the commission of inquiry into Pikoli's fitness to hold office. During his testimony before the Ginwala Commission, Pikoli said he believed that his suspension amounted to political interference, as it happened soon after he told Mbeki and Mabandla that he had received the warrants to arrest Selebi and was about to execute them.

The Ginwala Commission praised Pikoli as a person of 'unimpeach-able integrity'.[11] However, it also found that his refusal of Mbeki's request for a two-week postponement amounted to a failure on his part to appreciate sensitivities around national security and showed a lack of respect for the president's constitutional obligation to maintain stability and national security. It noted that Pikoli believed his own assessment of national security was superior to that of the president.

By the time the Ginwala Commission concluded its work, Mbeki had resigned as president and Kgalema Motlanthe was acting president. Consequently, it was Motlanthe who received the Ginwala Commission's report. In one of the most consequential decisions of his interim presidency, Motlanthe decided not to reinstate Pikoli as the NDPP. GCIS did not get too involved in the communication drama that unfolded at this point and left the matter largely to the Department of Justice and Motlanthe's communication team.

The Ginwala Commission took place against the backdrop of the debate around the future of the Scorpions, which fell under Pikoli as the NDPP. A section of the ANC believed that the Scorpions were waging a political campaign against some leaders of the ANC and accused Mbeki of using the Scorpions and other state institutions against Jacob Zuma, who had been dismissed as deputy president on 14 June 2005.

One of the key resolutions adopted at the ANC national conference at Polokwane in December 2007 was that the Scorpions should be disbanded. This must be one of the most efficiently implemented policy resolutions in the ANC's history. Ten months later, in October 2008, the Scorpions were officially disbanded by Parliament. If a similar commitment and single-minded focus were adopted to, say, eliminate bucket toilets in schools, implement poverty alleviation measures or build houses, just imagine what could be achieved.

It would be years before I would find out what Pikoli had whispered to me that day at Mahlamba Ndlopfu. I ran into him in February 2020 at a dinner to which President Cyril Ramaphosa had invited a number of former directors-general. I finally had the courage to ask him. 'You are about to be thrown into the eye of the storm,' he had apparently said to me, knowing that I would be told to announce his suspension. I welcomed this revelation, as it erased the awkwardness I had felt whenever I bumped into him in the years after we both had left the public service.

7

Two centres of power

A YEAR BEFORE I was appointed as head of GCIS, something happened that would change the course of South Africa's history for ever through its indirect consequences. On 2 June 2005, Schabir Shaik, a Durban businessman and financial advisor to then Deputy President Jacob Zuma, was found guilty on two counts of corruption and one count of fraud and sentenced to 15 years in prison. During the trial, heard by Judge Hilary Squires in the Durban High Court, it emerged that Shaik had a corrupt relationship with Zuma in that he had paid Zuma hundreds of thousands of rands in exchange for political influence in the multibillion-rand arms deal (1999).

Two weeks later, on 14 June, Mbeki relieved Zuma of his duties as deputy president, after which Zuma resigned as an MP. In the aftermath of the Shaik trial, Zuma was formally charged with corruption by the NPA. Lengthy legal proceedings ensued, and Zuma's efforts to delay or avoid prosecution went on for many years. Zuma and French arms company Thales still face charges of fraud, corruption, money laundering and racketeering linked to the arms deal.

Mbeki's decision to fire Zuma triggered a power struggle within the ANC that continues to this day. Many ANC members and leaders never accepted Mbeki's decision, and this created divisions that brought out the worst form of factionalism in the organisation's history. Almost overnight, the ANC was divided into two factions: those who supported Mbeki and those who backed Zuma. What made it worse was that some of the Zuma supporters gave an ethnic slant to the emerging factionalism and went as far as shamelessly printing and wearing T-shirts bearing the slogan '100% Zuluboy', suggesting that Zuma was being persecuted because he was Zulu.

After his sacking as deputy president, Zuma informed the ANC that he wanted to resign as deputy president of the ANC. However, just two weeks later, at a meeting of the ANC's National General Council (NGC) – the party's mid-term review conference – Zuma's decision to resign as deputy leader of the party was rejected. Shortly afterwards, Zuma and his supporters started a campaign to get Zuma elected as the next president of the ANC at the party's 52nd national conference, scheduled to take place in Polokwane in December 2007.

This was the first time I saw a closing of the ranks within the ANC. Even though many ministers and ANC comrades realised the seriousness of the situation and the impact of the Squires judgment, they weren't willing to call Zuma out and take action against him. At the time, this turn of events left me deeply uncomfortable, and I had to ask myself whether the ANC would ever be the same again.

Over the next two years, several attempts were made by various ANC leaders to unite the party and convince Mbeki not to contest the presidency (while Mbeki's term as president of the republic was limited by the Constitution, there was no term limit on the ANC presidency). A belief took root that Mbeki might, upon re-election as ANC leader, use his position as party leader to remain the power behind the throne.[12] Even though a motion was carried at the ANC policy conference in Midrand in June 2007 that 'the leader of the ANC should preferably also be the leader of the country', Mbeki decided to go ahead and stand for ANC president.[13]

The weeks leading up to the Polokwane conference were characterised by all manner of rumour-mongering and speculation, largely because it was the first time the position of president of the ANC had been contested – and highly contested at that. I attended the conference not as a card-carrying member but as a so-called deployed cadre, a term used to describe ANC members who were in senior government positions.

When I arrived in Polokwane, I stopped for a drink at a popular spot on the outskirts of the city and this was where I got my first taste of the hostility the conference would become known for. I was met by a group of delegates who wasted no time in hurling insults at me for being an 'Mbeki-ite' and telling me in isiZulu, 'Isikhathi senu sesiphelile zinjandini' (Your time is up, dogs). I wasn't sure how safe I would be if I stayed there, so I decided to leave and go straight to my hotel.

I had attended all the ANC conferences since the party was unbanned in 1990 but I had never before experienced the kind of animosity and tension that was present in Polokwane. Usually, delegates would sing struggle songs, and I had looked forward to joining in, but what I encountered was what could only be described as factional singing, with groups in different parts of the venue singing different songs as if to out-sing one another. Each faction sang songs in support of their own candidate. It was quite chaotic, with people shouting and shuffling about; there was little discipline or tolerance and at one point I feared the large marquee might collapse.

Some of the delegates neither realised nor cared that the event was being broadcast live. The factional singing set a negative tone for the rest of the conference, and it took Mosiuoa 'Terror' Lekota, ANC chairperson at the time, several attempts to get the gathering to settle down, as some of the delegates made it clear that they didn't recognise his authority. There were scenes of disruption at every point and even a call for Lekota to step down as chairperson because he was accused of being biased. At that point I was ashamed of and embarrassed by my ANC membership – strange feelings for someone who had spent his adult life in the movement.

Tensions continued to rise and the leadership, itself divided, was unable to control the situation. During the breaks, I realised that while I recognised most of the songs, their style and the dancing of some of the delegates were different to what I was accustomed to. It made me doubt whether some of the delegates were true ANC members. They danced and sang more like members of the Inkatha Freedom Party, and they sang louder than everyone else. This was helped by the fact that the Zuma faction had the most delegates; KwaZulu-Natal was the largest province in the ANC at the time.

What saved the conference was the fact that the outcome of the election of the top six party leaders was announced on the second day. This calmed the mood because the Zuma faction had the most candidates and felt that they had achieved a key objective. Although this didn't stop the heckling and unruly behaviour during the plenary sessions, some semblance of order returned as the newly elected leaders took charge of the proceedings.

I was also intrigued by how the ANC conference commission discussions, where policy debates were meant to take place, were muted after the top six positions were announced. There were more delegates singing outside the venues where the commission discussions were taking place than inside. I got the distinct sense that some of the delegates had come to the conference only to vote, and had no interest in the policy discussions, because the voting for the other positions took place in parallel to the commission discussions. Watching these events unfold and bumping into groups of 'singers' hurling insults at whoever they considered to be a member of another faction was unbearable.

I left the conference on day two, and on the way home I shed a tear for the movement I loved. I wondered whether the ANC would ever be the same again. Watching the rest of the conference on television, like the rest of the country, I considered it to be something resembling a circus. At the end of the conference Zuma triumphed by 2 329 votes to 1 505 and became the new leader of the ANC, with

Kgalema Motlanthe as his deputy. This hailed the start of the period of two centres of power, since Mbeki was still president of the country.

In 2008 Zuma challenged the decision to prosecute him for corruption following the Shaik judgment. On Friday 12 September of that year Judge Chris Nicholson found that the corruption charges against Zuma were unlawful on procedural grounds. In his judgment Nicholson also said that he believed there had been political interference in the timing of the charges brought against Zuma. (Nicholson's ruling was later overturned by the Supreme Court of Appeal.)

The climate in the ANC had become very toxic, and after the Nicholson judgment a number of party leaders were baying for Mbeki's blood. The Zuma faction used the judgment as the smoking gun in support of their argument that Mbeki had long been using state institutions to fight his political battles with Zuma.

The following Friday, 19 September, the ANC's National Executive Committee (NEC) met to debate how to deal with this development. On Saturday morning, news reports quoted anonymous ANC sources suggesting that, after hours of deliberation and debate, the NEC had decided to recall Mbeki. I started to receive requests from the media for comment about the recall, and I tried to get confirmation first from Essop Pahad, but his cellphones were off. When I also could not reach the Reverend Frank Chikane or Mukoni Ratshitanga, Mbeki's spokesperson at the time, all I could do was refer journalists to the ANC and the Presidency.

The NEC sent a delegation, led by Motlanthe, to Mahlamba Ndlopfu that afternoon to inform Mbeki of the NEC's decision to recall him.[14] Clearly, two centres of power were operating on that fateful weekend – the ANC NEC sitting in Kempton Park and the Presidency in Pretoria. This presented a classical communication nightmare.

Later that day, Ratshitanga and I eventually connected and were able to decide on a communication strategy. I realised that the communication environment was about to change quite radically, but for the moment I kept at a distance from these issues as it was largely a party-political storm and not a government matter.

Mbeki decided that he was not going to contest the ANC's decision, but he wanted to ensure that the process was managed in accordance with the Constitution. He convened a special meeting of the Cabinet for the following day. At the meeting, Mbeki informed the ministers that there was no provision in the Constitution for him to be recalled as president but that he was willing to resign. This was true leadership, in my view. He could simply have rejected the NEC decision as unlawful, but he felt that it was not in the interest of our young democracy, or of the ANC, to create a constitutional crisis.

The Cabinet meeting, which I attended, was tense and emotional, with many ministers struggling to hide their feelings. Interestingly, a number of ministers were also NEC members and had been part of the meeting where the decision had been taken to recall Mbeki, but in terms of the ANC culture they had to abide by the decision of the majority. Cabinet expressed unhappiness and regret at the NEC's decision but supported Mbeki's decision to resign. Several ministers also wanted to know what the implication of Mbeki's resignation would be for them, since he had appointed them to Cabinet. My recollection is that Mbeki advised them to wait for the ANC to decide on their future.

On a personal level, it was very painful for me to watch the party of Mandela, Sisulu, Tambo and Slovo tear itself apart. I could not understand why the NEC felt it necessary to remove Mbeki with only a few months left before the 2009 general election, after which he would have stepped down anyway. The decision seemed to be driven by vindictiveness and hatred of Mbeki the man, and party interests were prioritised above those of the country. This was not the ANC I knew and had risked my life to join.

Ratshitanga and I were then asked to liaise with the SABC for the president to address the nation after the Cabinet meeting. Mbeki told

us what he wanted to say and the brief statement was typed up. Ratshitanga and I rushed to the SABC studios in Pretoria to ensure that
everything was in place. When he arrived at the studios, the president
looked extremely glum and from my observation seemed to be holding back tears. Mbeki delivered his message, and when he was finished
he wanted to be out of the studio as quickly as possible. One sentence
from his statement has stayed with me: 'I depart this office knowing
that many men and women in South Africa have worked to achieve
better lives for all.'

The next few days were rather unsettling, with so many things up in
the air. I felt obliged to keep the public and the public service informed
about the unfolding events to assure everyone that the country wasn't
falling apart. The Presidency also tried to keep the public informed,
but in the absence of a clear and coordinated communications strategy
from GCIS and the Presidency, the primary source of information
became leaks, anonymous sources and a lot of speculation, which
created much uncertainty.

Although some ministers had mentioned the idea of resigning en
masse from Cabinet as soon as Mbeki's resignation became effective,
no formal decision was made in this regard, and if there was, I was not
aware of it. My team and I continued to monitor the story as it unfolded, and, in my idealism, I was hoping that an opportunity would
arise for GCIS and the Presidency to create an overall communication strategy. Also, it would have been preferable to align our messag-
ing with that of the ANC communicators, but this never happened.

The following week, I was having lunch with a friend at a restaurant
in Pretoria when my phone rang. It was a journalist inquiring whether
it was true that a number of ministers had resigned. My heart almost
jumped out of my chest as I was not aware of this development.
Then Lesetja Kganyago, the director-general at National Treasury,
called to say that he had also just heard that a number of ministers,

including finance minister Trevor Manuel, had resigned. He told me that Manuel could not be reached by phone because he was on a flight to New York. Kganyago's concern was twofold: first, Manuel was likely to be ambushed by the media when he arrived in New York; and, second, he was concerned about the impact this would have on the South African currency.

I alerted my media team while I tried to investigate the matter. To my great surprise, the media already had a list of the ministers who had allegedly resigned. I immediately called Frank Chikane and asked that he help me establish whether the news was true. Although he knew some ministers were contemplating resigning from Cabinet, Chikane told me he was not aware that they had taken such a decision. Apparently some ministers, such as Manuel, thought that the Cabinet should resign as a collective, while others felt it should be left to individuals to decide what they wanted to do.

When Chikane got back to me, he confirmed that there was indeed no collective decision on the matter. The ministers understood that they were not legally obliged to resign simply because the person who had appointed them had left office. According to Section 94 of the Constitution, 'the Cabinet, the Deputy President, Ministers and any Deputy Ministers remain competent to function until the person elected President by the next Assembly assumes office'.

My primary issue was the fact that I had to learn about the resignations through the media, which meant another communications crisis was unfolding in front of my eyes. I felt completely powerless and let down by my superiors.

Kganyago and I agreed to send a text message to Manuel so that he would be prepared to face the media when he arrived in New York. A few hours later, we received confirmation that some ministers had indeed resigned but had not authorised the publication of the story. In fact, when we got hold of Manuel, it emerged that he had written a resignation letter and left it with the president's office in case he was required to resign while he was overseas.

In the end, it turned out that a sizeable number of ministers were very unhappy with the ANC NEC decision to recall Mbeki and decided to resign in solidarity with Mbeki and as a sign of protest against the NEC. Other ministers resigned because they assumed that their term would come to an end as soon as Mbeki left office. Even Manuel was unclear about the constitutional position and was among those who thought his term would end when Mbeki left office. He eventually withdrew his resignation letter when he learnt that it was not a constitutional requirement.

President Thabo Mbeki's Cabinet secretariat and support staff. Joel Netshitenzhe and I are on the far left, in the front row, and on Mbeki's left are Frank Chikane and Essop Pahad. On Mbeki's right is Phumzile Mlambo-Ngcuka, deputy president.

In the end, 11 members of Mbeki's Cabinet resigned after Kgalema Motlanthe was sworn in as caretaker president: Phumzile Mlambo-Ngcuka (deputy president), Trevor Manuel (finance), Essop Pahad (minister in the Presidency), Ronnie Kasrils (intelligence), Ngconde Balfour (correctional services), Alec Erwin (public enterprises), Mosibudi Mangena (science and technology), Thoko Didiza (public works), Sydney Mufamadi (provincial and local government), Mosiuoa Lekota, (defence) and Geraldine Fraser-Moleketi (public service and administration).

I never anticipated that the end of Mbeki's presidency would be this messy and potentially damaging to the democratic project. I tried to stay in close contact with Chikane to stay abreast of developments but mostly I felt like I was playing catch-up all the time. He and his team in the Presidency were so overwhelmed that they overlooked the importance of communicating information around this transition period. Ironically, I found myself relying quite heavily on my media contacts to understand what was happening. I still joke with my journalist friends about how, for once, they became my sources instead of my being their source of information.

After Mbeki's resignation, Kgalema Motlanthe was elected as president by Parliament on 25 September 2008. He served in this position for the next seven months, until the general election in April 2009. I first met Motlanthe when I was a student and UDF activist, and I enjoyed working under him when he became president. His staff were always welcoming and seemed to understand the strategic nature of my job, and I could always reach him by telephone whenever an urgent need arose. Unlike many of the leaders elected at Polokwane, Motlanthe was a calm and reflective person who held neither grudges nor ill-feeling against anyone who might not have voted for him at the 2007 conference.

Even though Motlanthe would only be president for a short time, and the country desperately needed some political stability, he had no choice but to appoint a new Cabinet due to the number of ministers who had resigned. When Motlanthe announced the new Cabinet at a media briefing, I almost fell off the chair when I heard that Dr Manto Tshabalala-Msimang was going to be the new minister in the Presidency and my boss at GCIS. Now I'm definitely going to be fired, I thought. The thing is, Tshabalala-Msimang and I had a little bit of history.

When Tshabalala-Msimang was minister of health in the Mbeki administration, she became controversial for her views on the treatment of HIV/Aids. A media storm broke when she attended the XVI International AIDS Conference in Toronto, Canada, in August 2006, where she again promoted her view that traditional medicines and nutritious African foods were sufficient to prevent HIV.[15] She also displayed a plethora of vegetables, including garlic, at South Africa's exhibition stand at the conference.

At that point I had only been in the GCIS job for a few months, and I had the thankless task of managing the government's response to the matter. We decided to focus on communicating the message that government was providing the largest antiretroviral (ARV) drug programme in the world and that this was based on an acceptance of the fact that HIV causes Aids. We also said that although a healthy diet was an important part of the programme, it should not be to the exclusion of ARV therapy. Tshabalala-Msimang interpreted this to mean that the government in general and GCIS in particular were throwing her under the bus, so to speak. As I was the bearer of this message, she would refuse to talk to me when we passed each other in government corridors or met at functions.

However, after her appointment to the Presidency she told me that since she knew nothing about communication, she wanted to focus on other responsibilities in the Presidency and would leave all communication matters to me. I had expected her to be bitter and angry towards me, but we went on to have a solid working relationship based on mutual respect and cooperation in the few months we worked together (she passed away in December 2009). I found her to be not effective as minister in charge of government communication, because her relationship with the media was broken, and I welcomed the fact that she gave me the full mandate to work with the media. She detested journalists, blaming them for tarnishing her image during the HIV/Aids saga.

Under Motlanthe I had to deal with another challenging communication dilemma. In March 2009 the Dalai Lama, the exiled Tibetan spiritual leader, was refused a visa to visit South Africa to attend a peace conference in Johannesburg. The Chinese government is on record as saying that governments who entertain the Dalai Lama risk breaking any possible relationship with Beijing. A number of ministers, including Barbara Hogan, the new minister of health, made it known that they were not happy with the visa decision. Tshabalala-Msimang was furious and she instructed me to issue a statement condemning those ministers and distancing government from Hogan's comments.

As if that was not enough, I was invited onto a programme on Radio 702 with the minister. I hated every minute of it. Here I was, debating and disagreeing with a Cabinet member in public. As I had huge respect and admiration for Barbara, this was particularly difficult for me and I regret it to this day.

When Jacob Zuma assumed office on 9 May 2009 it marked the beginning of the end of a close relationship between me, as government spokesperson, and the Presidency. I have no memories of one-on-one meetings with Zuma as I never succeeded in securing any such meetings with him.

Where I was often able to steal a moment with Mbeki or Motlanthe after Cabinet meetings to seek guidance on a Cabinet decision, Zuma was always either in a rush to the next meeting or would refer me to Collins Chabane, the newly appointed minister in the Presidency (my third minister in three years). I soon got the message that my requests for meetings were not welcome and so I stopped pursuing them.

Despite my lack of access to Zuma, Chabane's appointment marked the beginning of a solid partnership and friendship. I had met Chabane in several ANC meetings prior to the 1994 elections and I had come to know him as a comrade. He was unassuming and, like his predecessors, trusted me to do my job, and also did not ask me to show him Cabinet statements prior to their release. As a member of the NEC, Chabane briefed me on the outcomes of NEC meetings so that I would have the necessary context for decisions that would eventually become government policy. Both Chabane and I were enthusiastic golfers and we spent many hours discussing life and politics on golf courses around Gauteng.

During the Zuma era, Cabinet no longer commented on current affairs matters as they arose outside of Cabinet meetings. Several attempts to get Zuma's views on such issues were unsuccessful. This made my task as government spokesperson increasingly difficult because I went to face the media at the post-Cabinet briefing sessions not knowing the president's views on the matters of the day.

Nothing is more difficult for a communicator than operating in an environment where you don't have access to your principal. There were instances where I had to chair media briefings following major announcements by Zuma, such as the appointment of Cabinet members, and would only get copies of the statement prepared by his team a few minutes before the media briefing. The practice we had put in place during the Mbeki era, where I would meet the president at least an hour ahead of the media briefing to discuss the statement and identify possible questions from the media and suggest responses for the president, fell away. Perhaps Zuma held such pre-briefing sessions with his own team, but he did not with me.

I soon got the impression that directors-general who had been part of Mbeki's administration were automatically perceived as part of the Mbeki faction and so were regarded with mistrust. However, when I went to the office in the morning I did so to serve and be loyal to the Constitution, not to advance the needs of a specific faction within the ANC. I regarded myself as a professional civil servant whose responsibility was to serve all the citizens of the country, irrespective of their political affiliation. The generation of directors-general that

I served with during Madiba's and Mbeki's time were all professional administrators who owed their allegiance to the Constitution.

Presenting the GCIS annual report to Parliament's portfolio committee with members of the GCIS Exco, Nebo Legoabe (right) and Phumla Williams (back).

Although most of us were ANC members who saw our role in government as a continuation of a journey to liberate our people from the legacy of colonialism and apartheid, we never saw ourselves as part of this or that faction. We were committed to serving under anyone who was chosen by the democratic processes of the ruling party to lead the country. I found it extremely regrettable that some individuals who were appointed to ministerial positions after 2009 treated many of the existing directors-general with suspicion simply because we happened to have worked for the Mbeki administration. As a consequence, the civil service lost a vast number of competent and qualified administrators, who left because they were not trusted by some of the new ministers who came into government.

During the Mbeki era, directors-general were invited to and participated in most of the NEC subcommittees to provide technical support to the policy processes taking place within the ruling party. For instance, when I was director-general in the Department of Public Works I routinely participated in the Economic Transformation Committee and also served on the Communications Committee of the ANC NEC. When I joined GCIS I was also invited to attend NEC meetings as an observer. There was a level of trust between civil administrators and their political heads and an understanding that our technical skills could add value to the policy-making processes.

Soon, though, I found myself receiving fewer and fewer invitations to these meetings. I recall an incident sometime in 2010 when I was invited to an NEC subcommittee meeting at the ANC head office in Luthuli House, in downtown Johannesburg. I got into the lift and as it was about to close a number of ANC Youth League members, including Julius Malema, jumped in. He first looked at me and then turned to face the lift door before saying, 'Babatlang mo, nako yabona ifedile' (What do they want here, their time is up).

I didn't take the comment seriously and joined in the laughter that ensued. But when I entered the subcommittee meeting, I got a very hostile reception, and it dawned on me that I was no longer welcome at these events. I soon stopped attending.

These changes cannot be attributed solely to Zuma and should also be ascribed to the attitude of a larger group of leaders who felt that their time had come to take charge of the levers of power. The distrust of civil servants from the Mbeki era and the 'it's our turn' attitude became two key characteristics of the political leadership of the Zuma years.

Under Zuma, Cabinet lekgotlas ran like clockwork because all ministerial clusters soon realised that everything they presented would be approved. The Mbeki-type scrutiny was no longer there.

I sensed that the voices of directors-general were getting quieter or slightly muted, as challenging or disagreeing with the newly appointed ministers could lead to their contracts being terminated. There was an unprecedented exit of skilled people, which was enough to worry anyone who was concerned about service delivery issues. The directors-general who left were replaced by less experienced individuals. I was becoming something of a rare bird, as I had been in the system since 1994.

A report published in 2017 by the Institute of Race Relations found that a total of 172 new directors-general were appointed between 2009 and 2017. On average a director-general spent 22 months in office before being replaced. According to the same report, a total of 62 ministerial and 63 deputy ministerial positions, and one change to the deputy presidency, were reshuffled in the same period. In the end only 11 people from the 2009 Cabinet remained in office by the end of 2017.[16]

Experience and expertise no longer counted for anything. No private company or public administration can maintain a high level of efficiency with such a high turnover of leadership. Needless to say, this led to great uncertainty and instability in the civil service.

During his nine years as president, Zuma reshuffled his Cabinet no fewer than 12 times. Changes in political leadership were often accompanied by changes in the structure of government departments. Zuma didn't seem to appreciate the time it took to move functions and personnel from one department to another. In the process, valuable planning and implementation time was lost.

Furthermore, because many of the ministers did not trust the senior civil servants in their departments when they assumed office, any advice or criticism offered by these civil servants was easily interpreted as defiance. There was also very little in terms of a formal process of handing over to a new incumbent on a ministerial level. In some instances, officials would prepare handover reports for the new ministers, but these reports often found their way into a filing cabinet never to be read. In effect, the frequent changes in Cabinet were bound to – and did – affect the capacity of the state to deliver on its mandate of serving citizens.

Although the lack of clarity regarding the different roles of ministers and administrators in the public service did not begin with the Zuma administration, it became more pronounced during his tenure due to the number of Cabinet reshuffles. A number of the new ministers wanted to stamp their authority on their departments, and this often entailed the introduction of new policy and strategy regimes.

Many of the conflicts between political leaders and their directors-general could also be attributed to ministers' wanting to have a greater say in procurement processes. Some didn't understand their role vis-à-vis that of the accounting officer of the respective department. I had many conversations with directors-general who were very unhappy with the way their new political bosses thought they could simply give procurement instructions without realising that procurement processes involved compliance. Whenever a group of directors-general gathered, a central theme would often be how they felt unwanted and mistrusted by the new administration.

We also shared stories about some of their extravagances. For instance, some ministers refused to use items such as cars, furniture and even cutlery for the simple reason that those items had been used by their predecessors. Others even organised cleansing ceremonies before they would set foot in their new offices. This too had already started under Mbeki. When I was with the Department of Public Works, my team often had to arrange for furniture to be replaced and stored or new carpets to be put in.

I observed that policy uncertainty was starting to creep into a number of areas, especially in the economic cluster. This led to turf wars between the ministries of finance, trade and industry, economic development and planning (the last-mentioned housed in the Presidency). As part of what seemed to be a purge of Mbeki supporters, the PCAS unit in the Presidency was also shut down. The unit had been responsible for government-wide planning and for ensuring that there was proper coordination of policy processes in government. The effect was that the heads of the different departments, especially in the economic cluster, would make opposing policy pronouncements, with a devastating effect on policy certainty.

The role of National Treasury was neutralised, and many of the new ministers felt emboldened to make policy pronouncements before confirming whether the fiscus had the funds. Moreover, the Presidential Working Groups, established by Mbeki to improve cooperation with the private sector, ceased to meet and were eventually abandoned. The relationship between business and government deteriorated further, spurred by the introduction of concepts such as white monopoly capital, which projected business as the enemy of transformation. This language also found its way into government processes, as Zuma and certain ministers started using the white-monopoly-capital rhetoric in public utterances.

Things also started going wrong in the boards that were appointed to SOEs such as Eskom, Transnet and others. It would later come to light that the Guptas had a hand in getting certain people appointed to these boards. Although the appointments of CEOs of SOEs still required Cabinet approval, it later emerged that the Guptas often hand-picked individuals who were close to them. I was quite shocked when I learnt that people I once respected had been appointed to such positions on the strength of Gupta recommendations.

As a result, corporate governance soon started to fail, which led to many of the SOEs performing dismally and having to rely on numerous bail-outs from the fiscus, at the expense of other pressing needs in education, health and housing. It was sad to see the revolution being derailed in this manner by people who once belonged to the liberation movement.

On 29 October 2009 I set off for an IMC board meeting in Houghton, Johannesburg. On my arrival, I was confronted by a visibly upset

Wendy Luhabe, a highly respected and prominent Johannesburg businesswoman who was the chairperson of the board.

'Themba, what is going on?' she asked.

I had no idea what she was referring to and asked her to explain.

'Haven't you heard? We have all been dismissed and a new board has been appointed!'

I couldn't hide my shock and embarrassment. I was the accounting officer for the board, but this important decision had been taken by the Presidency without my input or knowledge. Some of the board members had already arrived for the meeting, so I asked to be excused to try and figure out what was going on. First I tried to reach Collins Chabane, but without success. Then I called my office to check the information with the Presidency. After a few minutes, it was confirmed: the Presidency had dismissed the board and issued a statement announcing the appointment of a new board.

I still couldn't believe it was possible and asked my office to email me a copy of the statement. But there it was, in black and white. With my tail between my legs, I entered the boardroom and asked to see Luhabe privately for a few seconds. I confirmed the news of the board's dismissal and apologised profusely.

There was a tense atmosphere when Luhabe and I walked back into the room. I struggled to maintain eye contact with the other board members, who included CEOs of large companies, some of them listed on the Johannesburg Stock Exchange, and other government officials, such as the directors-general of tourism and international relations. They served on the board on a voluntary basis and didn't receive compensation for it. The board members were equally shocked and disappointed at the news. I also apologised to them and expressed my regret for what had happened and for the manner in which the Presidency had handled the matter.

I decided to break ranks and tell them that I had been neither consulted nor informed about the decision. Although the Presidency had the authority to appoint the members of the IMC board, the least it could have done was to formally notify the sitting board members of its intention to appoint a new board and to have a proper handover, or at the very least to thank them for their services.

I struggled to understand how something like this was possible. When I finally spoke to Chabane, he acknowledged that the correct procedure had not been followed and agreed to draft a letter on behalf of the president to apologise for not communicating with the board members through the proper channels. Wendy Luhabe wrote a letter to the Presidency to express her disappointment about the way in which the matter had been dealt with, saying, among other things, 'I felt unappreciated and discarded.'

Incidentally, one of the first items on the agenda when the new board of trustees met was to discuss the fees/stipends for members. I had to give them a lengthy explanation about why IMC board membership was on a voluntary basis; apparently, the new members had not been informed of this prior to their appointment, and some were less than impressed. Several of the new board members did not have full-time jobs and would struggle to serve on a voluntary basis. We eventually decided to cover at least the travel costs of board members, even though these costs were not budgeted for.

The new board was subsequently inaugurated. To my surprise, no members of the dismissed board were reappointed, except for Ajay Gupta, who I could not remember ever attending a board meeting up to that point.[17]

During this time, my ability to direct and influence communication messages became severely constrained. The limited access I now had with the ANC head office and NEC Communications Committee meant that my role had shifted. I no longer had the ability to be part of the process of developing party messages to ensure alignment between party and government communications. In some ways, the notion of two centres of power was amplified by the very people who, before the Polokwane conference, had advocated for one centre of power as part of their argument to stop Mbeki from securing a third term as ANC president.

8

The Saxonwold summons

IN JUNE-JULY 2010 South Africa hosted the FIFA World Cup, becoming the first African country to stage this global sporting event. I was intensively involved with the communications and marketing task teams for the World Cup and also played a role through my involvement with the International Marketing Council (IMC).

In January of that year, the IMC undertook to market South Africa at the 2010 World Economic Forum (WEF) meeting in Davos, Switzerland. One of our major concerns at the time was the lack of a common message from South Africans who had attended previous WEF meetings, and we wanted to ensure that all business and government leaders spoke with one voice ahead of the World Cup.

GCIS and the IMC prepared key messages that were endorsed by Cabinet and business organisations, and we prepared marketing materials and brochures to be given to all South Africans who would be at Davos. We also produced a scarf in the colours of the South African flag, which became the hottest item at Davos that year and could be seen in every corner of the town. The demand was so high that we had to order additional scarves, which had to be flown in from Johannesburg.

We organised a number of fora that were addressed by South African

Top: *With FIFA president, Sepp Blatter (left), at an event in Sandton ahead of the 2010 FIFA World Cup.*
Bottom: *Addressing communicators at a government communicators' workshop in Pretoria.*

business and government leaders, all of which were oversubscribed. We managed to secure interviews with our ministers and business leaders by all the major international news networks. Generally, a very positive impression of brand South Africa was created at Davos, and we felt we had helped to put South Africa on the map as an emerging economy with great prospects for investment.

The GCIS and IMC team was over the moon and our flight back home was one of the most memorable trips I've ever had. I was incredibly proud to call myself a South African when the World Cup turned out to be a great success.

After the replacement of the IMC board in October 2009, I remained as one of the three government representatives. Ajay Gupta also remained on the board, having been first nominated in 2002 by Essop Pahad. (Although Pahad is reportedly the person who introduced the Gupta family to the ANC leadership, he denies this. According to Pahad when he met the Gupta brothers they already had relationsips with certain ANC leaders.)

As Ajay had not attended previous board meetings, I only met him for the first time in March 2010. At that time the IMC was working with the Department of International Relations and Cooperation (as the Department of Foreign Affairs was renamed in 2009) on the plans for President Zuma's upcoming state visit to India. During the meeting Ajay was very forthright and positioned himself as the key person who would be facilitating the business delegation. He made it clear that he had discussed the trip with Zuma and that he would be the contact person between the South African delegation and the Indian government and businesses.

I found this highly irregular as I had never heard of a private individual being the main contact between two governments on a state visit. I was also surprised that someone who had missed all board meetings in the previous months was now claiming such a position for himself. However, I didn't challenge this behaviour at the time. My sole mandate was to align the communication messages between government and the business delegation. It was not my place to comment on what was a matter between the Presidency and the Department of International Relations and Cooperation.

Later, it emerged that many of the business leaders who were part of the delegation to India were also unhappy about the role played by Ajay on the visit. Their impression was that he became the main coordinator and facilitator of meetings between the South African delegation and the Indian delegations. Ordinarily, the ministries of international relations, finance and trade and industry would play this role.

Shortly after our first encounter in March, Ajay started pestering me about setting up a meeting to discuss a proposal he had. In May he invited me to his house in Saxonwold, and it was on the day set for our meeting that I got the call from President Zuma (described in Chapter 1) during which he said, 'My brother, there are these Gupta men, I want you to meet with them and help them.'

The meeting with Ajay Gupta in Saxonwold left me upset and deeply perturbed. When I left the Gupta compound that day, part of me wanted to drive to Luthuli House to seek a meeting with Gwede Mantashe, then secretary-general of the ANC. But I wondered what that would achieve, since it would mean laying a complaint against not only the president of the ANC but also the president of the country.

I decided to reach out to a few friends instead. The best advice I got was that I should report the matter to my superior. So I called Collins Chabane and told him what had just happened. He was as shocked as I was and undertook to investigate the matter.

I also contacted the Reverend Frank Chikane, whom I considered to be a mentor and in whom I often confided, to seek his advice and guidance. Chikane was very troubled when he heard about my ordeal and he also advised me to report the incident to Chabane. I had always respected Chikane's commitment to the Constitution and his attention to detail in matters of state. He was unrelenting when it came to following procedure, and his ability to work with and earn the respect of Cabinet ministers from all factions of the ANC was admirable.

The more I thought about the Saxonwold meeting, the more depressed I felt. I hoped that I would feel better after talking to trusted friends and colleagues, but my spirits remained low. I called Tamoledi Selane, a dear friend of mine, and he invited me over to his house for a drink. When I got home a few hours later, I did not have the courage to tell Phindile about my ordeal, and that night I didn't sleep a wink. I expected a call from the president at any moment to ask me about the outcome of the meeting or to reprimand me for refusing to cooperate with Ajay.

I woke up the next morning feeling demotivated and stressed. As I drove to my office in Pretoria, I debated whether to tell my team about what had happened. I eventually decided against it, since it could place the president in a very bad light.

I managed to secure a meeting with Chabane a few days later to establish whether he had done anything about the matter. He told me he had not had an opportunity to raise the issue with the president. I understood the dilemma he was facing: it would be very difficult for him to confront Zuma on such a sensitive matter. Chabane became a pillar of strength during this time, and there was never any doubt that he supported me in defying Ajay Gupta. I welcomed his assurance, even though I suspected the matter would require more than just his support.

I was convinced that Ajay was going to call Zuma. When, after a few weeks, I did not hear from Zuma again, I thought that either Ajay had not given him feedback on our meeting or he had got the feedback but was too angry to contact me.

In the next few weeks I also shared the details of my encounter

with Ajay with Deputy President Kgalema Motlanthe and Joel Netshitenzhe. Both of them were deeply shocked and disgusted by Ajay's
brazenness. They couldn't believe that he had said, through his close
ties to the president, that he could get ministers to do what he wanted.
A part of me wanted to believe that Ajay was simply using the president's name to achieve his nefarious objectives without Zuma's knowledge or permission.

Weeks and then several months passed without any further developments or any action being taken against me. I decided to put the
matter behind me and continue with my duties, which included
attending Cabinet meetings presided over by Zuma.

One of the most important tournaments on the South African golf-
ing calendar is the Nedbank Golf Challenge at Sun City. It is every
South African amateur golfer's dream to attend this annual tournament, and I made it a point to attend as often as possible. On Friday
3 December, in the late afternoon, my wife and I were on our way to
Sun City to attend the 2010 edition of the tournament; I was looking forward to a restful weekend and hoped to sneak in a round of
golf too.

Ordinarily, I switch off my mobile phone while driving, but that day
I had forgotten to do so. At around 6.30 pm, halfway through the trip,
my phone rang and I reluctantly took the call even though I didn't
recognise the number.

CALLER: Hi, Mr Maseko, sorry to disturb you after working hours.'
ME: 'No problem, who am I speaking to and how can I help you?'
CALLER: 'My name is Tony Gupta. I'm calling you from The New
    Age, a newspaper we are about to launch . . .'
ME: 'How can I help you?'
TONY: 'I'd like to have a meeting with you, urgently, to discuss
    government advertising in the newspaper because the launch

is happening very soon and we would like your assistance with the launch.'

ME: 'Okay, I don't mind meeting but could you please call me on Monday so that we can schedule an appointment via my office?'

TONY: 'Sorry, Mr Maseko, but the matter is very urgent and I would like to meet you as soon as possible.'

ME: 'Look Tony, I have an office to run and I know I have commitments on Monday morning, which I wouldn't like to change. Just call me on Monday morning and I'll see what I can do.'

TONY: 'Mr Maseko, can I come to the office on Monday morning at 8 o'clock and then we can find a slot in your diary?'

ME: 'Listen Tony, I'm driving now and I don't want to be rude but I can't continue this conversation with you at this moment, okay? Please call me on Monday.'

I put the phone down without waiting for his response.

'Who was that?' asked Phindile, who could hear that I had become increasingly annoyed with the call.

'It's some arrogant idiot who is demanding a meeting with me.'

I regretted taking the call but foolishly forgot to switch my mobile off. I was furious with myself when it rang again an hour or so later. But, always worried that a call might be urgent, I picked it up again.

CALLER: 'Good evening, Mr Maseko. This is Ajay speaking.'

ME: 'Good evening, Ajay.'

Ajay: 'I hear from my people that you are being difficult.'

ME: 'Ajay, that's not true. I tried to explain to your person that I was on the road and that he should call me on Monday to set up a meeting and—'

AJAY: 'It is very important that we meet you urgently because the matter we want to discuss can't wait.'

ME: 'Hold on, Ajay, I don't have a problem meeting you but—'

AJAY: 'No, no, no, this can't wait! In fact, we can't wait for Monday. Let's meet tomorrow at my house.'

ME: 'Listen Ajay, as I told your person, I'm on my way to Sun City and there is no way I can meet you tomorrow.'

AJAY: 'Listen to me carefully, okay . . . I am telling you that the meeting will take place tomorrow morning.'

ME: 'Now you listen to me, Ajay. You can't give me an instruction to meet you tomorrow because I don't work for you. Who do you think you are?'

AJAY: 'No, you listen! I will not tolerate any nonsense from you because you don't understand what's going on. I will speak to your superiors and tell them to replace you with someone who will be willing to cooperate.'

ME: 'You can go f*ck yourself then. I don't work for you!'

And with that I put the phone down, extremely angry and offended at Ajay's nerve. I don't know if my wife had ever heard me using such foul language on a business call. How could he call a senior government official and demand a meeting like that, as if he was my employer? I didn't know exactly what Ajay meant when he said he would speak to my superiors and have me replaced, but I took it as a direct threat.

I also couldn't help but think of Cabinet ministers like Tokyo Sexwale, then minister of housing, who had business interests in media companies such as the Times Media Group (which owned the *Sunday Times*, *Sowetan* and *Business Day*) but who had never made such demands.

The following week I spoke to Chabane about the two calls from the Gupta brothers. He surprised me by saying a number of individuals in government, including ministers, were also being harassed by the Guptas, who were apparently abusing their friendship with Zuma to make demands for many different things from different departments. I did not ask for further details. The less I knew the better, I thought.

Some of the people who I mentioned the calls to even suggested that I should lay a charge, but because I felt it was a political matter I hoped it could be resolved in a discussion between Chabane and the president.

In the following weeks, I started getting calls from a number of communicators in other national departments, complaining about the aggressive calls they were receiving from someone at *The New Age* who was demanding to meet with them. This person also gave the impression that I had given the green light for him to approach other officials. I made it very clear that I did not endorse the calls from *The New Age* but left it up to them to decide whether or not they wanted to meet with the representative.

This development gave me a sense that the Gupta brothers were getting desperate. On 6 December 2010, the first edition of *The New Age* was published.

9

Redeployed or fired?

IN LATE JANUARY 2011 – about seven months after my visit to the Guptas in Saxonwold and two months after Ajay's call to me while I was driving to Sun City – Nelson Mandela was admitted to the Milpark Hospital in Johannesburg. The 92-year-old Madiba had not been well for a long time and there were frequent rumours about his passing in the local and global media.

The Reverend Frank Chikane, when he was still director-general in the Presidency, put together a media and communications protocol to manage all communication pertaining to Mandela's health. This required us to communicate promptly to avoid any speculation in this regard, and included steps to be taken in the event of his passing. According to the protocol, the family would be informed of any developments regarding Mandela's health before any public announcement was made, and I had to manage all media engagements to protect the family from media pressure.

In the early hours of 26 January I received a call from Harold Maloka, a member of my GCIS communications team, who informed me that Madiba had been taken to hospital. I immediately set off for Milpark, and when I got there I was surprised to see a large number of media vehicles with satellite dishes and dozens of reporters already at the entrance. A number of police officers were controlling access to the hospital and I had to beg them to let me through as they were under strict instructions not to let anyone in.

As I entered the hospital building, I noticed that several of Madiba's family members had arrived and were being harassed by the media, who wanted an update on his health. Although I didn't get inside the ward where Madiba was receiving medical attention, I managed to speak to his ex-wife, Winnie Madikizela-Mandela, whom I was very close to at the time. She told me the doctors had assured the family that Madiba was responding well to the treatment he was receiving. I informed her that there was a huge media contingent outside that needed to be managed and the only way to do it would be to give an update on Madiba's condition.

At that time Jacob Zuma was in Davos, attending the WEF, and Kgalema Motlanthe was acting president. I was advised that Motlanthe was on his way to the hospital, and we decided to wait for his arrival and guidance before deciding how and when to communicate with the media. I found a quiet spot under the trees outside the hospital to gather my thoughts and take everything in. I started jotting down a possible statement, realising that the public in this case included the rest of the world, as members of the international media were in atten-dance. I also asked my team to check with the hospital management whether they had a large boardroom that we could use for a media briefing. We decided that the briefing should include medical staff, who would be better placed to explain Madiba's condition while re-specting his and the family's right to privacy.

Some of the family members were not pleased about our making details of Madiba's condition public, but we convinced them that the public and media interest was too great and that keeping silent would only fuel speculation. The family eventually agreed, on condition that not too much information be divulged and we included members of his medical team on the panel at the media briefing.

The next minute we heard loud police sirens, which meant that Motlanthe had arrived. As he entered the hospital foyer, I managed to grab his attention to discuss our suggestion for a media briefing. He had seen the media contingent outside the hospital and knew it would be impossible not to speak to them. Motlanthe suggested we do the media briefing within the hour. I then went outside and informed the media that we would be holding a media briefing soon. My team finalised the logistics and led the members of the media to the designated room so they could set up their equipment, as many of the media houses had told us they were planning to broadcast the media briefing live.

I spent a few minutes with the members of the medical team to get a sense of what they were prepared to say at the briefing, bearing in mind that we had to be sensitive to the family's concerns. After Motlanthe had spent some time with Madiba and his family, he left the ward. I briefed him on the talking points we had prepared and the proceedings, but as usual Motlanthe was more than happy with our plans and said, 'Let's go.'

When I entered the boardroom I could not believe my eyes. I had never seen so many journalists crammed into a single room. Motlanthe's security team had to squeeze him through to a table at the front, as some of the journalists were squatting on the floor. Microphones covered the surface of the table, some threatening to fall off. For the first time in my job as government spokesperson, I chaired a media briefing in which I did not recognise the majority of the journalists present.

After Motlanthe and a family member spoke, it was the turn of the medical specialist, who said Mandela was recovering very well for someone of his age and would be released within a matter of days. We also pleaded with the media to resist the temptation to spread rumours or harass members of the Mandela family. Motlanthe seemed pleased with everything and asked me to thank my team for a job well done.

Needless to say, most of the journalists remained camped outside the hospital premises until Madiba was discharged.

I decided to stick around the hospital because I didn't trust some of the journalists to comply with our request not to pester the family. I set up office in my car and conducted a number of interviews. Moments after I finally decided to go home, my phone rang – it was an international number. I was greeted by Lindiwe Sisulu, the minister of defence and military veterans, who sounded rather upset.

'Themba, what are you doing?' she asked abruptly.

'I'm at Milpark Hospital, where Madiba is being treated, minister. There was a media briefing,' I said, my mind racing as I tried to figure out what the call was about.

'Yes, that is why I'm calling. I'm with President Zuma in Davos and he is very unhappy about the briefing. Only the president is authorised to speak to the media about Madiba's health.'

I tried to explain the reasons why we had decided to address the media, and I also informed her that Motlanthe, in his role as acting president, had approved the media briefing. She told me in no uncertain terms that I had defied the president and that I should stop all media engagements about Madiba's health at once. The minister concluded the conversation by reminding me that she was conveying a direct instruction from Zuma and that my job was simply to comply.

I was both confused and taken aback by the call. As far as I was concerned, an acting president had the powers of the president, and not only had we consulted with Motlanthe but he had participated in the briefing. The way the system worked was that the principal conveys the main message and the communicators are then allowed to amplify the message because the principal cannot be expected – and indeed will not have the time – to conduct the great number of interviews that often follow a media briefing. We had followed the correct procedure.

However, it was not for me to go against the president's wishes, so I immediately cancelled the interviews I had lined up for the rest of the day. I became very concerned that I was in Zuma's bad books yet again, even if through no fault of my own. I recalled how, shortly after Zuma became president, some of his aides had spread rumours that I had apparently conspired with certain journalists to ask him difficult questions.

At GCIS, our practice was to give the SABC a slightly longer slot to ask questions since they are the public broadcaster and reach the majority of South Africans. This meant that Sophie Mokoena, at the time the political correspondent for the SABC, got more opportunity to ask questions. Our efforts to help the public broadcaster disseminate the news of the day to the majority of South Africans were apparently construed by Zuma's team as giving Sophie, in particular, an opportunity to undermine Zuma. They thought we were not doing enough to defend Zuma.

This was an indication that I was dealing with an administration that was suffering from the worst form of paranoia and saw everyone in government as pursuing an imaginary Mbeki-ite agenda. I couldn't believe that the Presidency could operate on this basis with GCIS, which was its own communication outfit, after all. I saw my responsibility as communicating government programmes and policies. It was the Presidency's job to communicate on matters pertaining to the president's office.

I heard about these rumours from one of my subordinates at GCIS, who also told me that Zuma's team was claiming that I was a member of the Congress of the People (COPE), the breakaway party established in December 2008 following Mbeki's recall as president. I was never a member of COPE. Zuma was set on getting rid of everyone he saw as a Mbeki supporter, and I can only assume that this was the reason for the rumours about me.

The rumours went so far that one day I got a call from a man who said he was calling from The Farm, as the headquarters of the NIA is known, and that he wanted to discuss an urgent matter with me. I obliged, even though the established protocol was that the director-general of the NIA would contact me directly if it was a matter of national importance.

I asked him to meet me at my office in Pretoria, but when he arrived 30 minutes late we didn't start off on a good foot. I asked him to get straight to the point of the meeting. I was surprised to notice that he looked a little anxious and lacked confidence. Then he proceeded to tell me in a very inarticulate way that The Farm was concerned about my role as CEO of GCIS because I wasn't doing enough to defend or protect President Zuma from media attacks and was allowing journalists such as Sophie Mokoena to grill him.

I immediately knew I was dealing with a rogue individual who could not have been authorised to have such a conversation with the accounting officer of a government department. I asked him to explain in greater detail. Mostly mumbling, he repeated how Zuma was under attack from the media and that GCIS was not doing anything about it. I realised that he had no clue what he was talking about. I stood up and asked him to go back to his office and write a formal letter to his director-general, who could then communicate their concerns to me in writing or ask his minister to raise these matters with my minister.

In my work as a civil servant in different government departments, I had never experienced such an amateurish and ridiculous interaction with a member of the intelligence community. I did not even bother to escalate the matter to Manana Manzini, the director-general of the NIA at the time.

While I was upset that false rumours were being spread about me, I decided to ignore them. I knew the real problem was that Zuma and his team had never understood the importance of preparing properly for a media briefing. Due to my lack of access to the president I could also never advise him or his team on any communication matters. In retrospect, I should have realised that an era of paranoia and mistrust was upon us. Today I know this was a warning of things to come.

The following Sunday afternoon – three days after the media briefing on Madiba's hospitalisation – I got a call from Collins Chabane. I assumed he wanted to invite me for a round of golf, but when he spoke it was in a serious tone. He asked that we meet first thing the next morning. I didn't ask for further details and only said I would be there at 8 am sharp.

When I walked into his office in the Union Buildings the following morning, I immediately sensed that something was up. He seemed tense and unsettled. Usually, we would sit informally around his board-room table, but this time he went to sit behind his desk, pointing me to the visitor's chair on the other side of it.

After exchanging the usual pleasantries he cut to the chase. He told me that Zuma had called him from Addis Ababa, where he was attending the African Union leaders' summit, to tell him that I should be removed from my position. 'The president says you should not be at GCIS by the time he gets back,' he said.

He apologised for being the bearer of bad news but said he had no choice but to implement the president's decision. I got a lump in my throat and slumped back into my chair. Chabane kept quiet for a few seconds to allow me to digest the news. I was at a complete loss for words. He went on to tell me that he neither understood nor agreed with the president but had no say in the matter.

'Did the president give reasons for the instruction?' I asked when I finally got my voice back.

'No, Themba, he did not . . . Look, I have really enjoyed working with you and I will try my best to find a position for you in another government department. Don't worry, I won't send you into the streets. I know you have not done anything wrong.'

We agreed to keep the matter between us until he found a new position for me. He wanted us to control the story in the media by announcing my move as a transfer rather than a dismissal. We briefly discussed the reasons for this turn of events. I told him I suspected that Zuma's instruction could have something to do with my acrimonious interactions with Ajay Gupta. We parted ways on the understanding that Chabane would speak to his Cabinet colleagues about the possibility of redeploying me to another department.

I was reeling when I left the Union Buildings. I debated whether to go to the office or drive home. I also thought of calling Phindile, but decided against it. I hoped Chabane could find me a new position before I broke the news to her. There were school fees, a bond and car instalments to be paid, and the possibility of my being unemployed would have only upset her. However, the president was due back the following day, which meant that my dismissal was imminent.

I eventually decided to go to the office but not to tell my staff anything. At the office, I tried my best to act as if nothing was wrong, but I asked my secretary to hold all my calls and to cancel all my meetings. I was so overwhelmed that a wave of exhaustion spilled over me. I later learnt that some of my staff members found me fast asleep in my office.

Later that day, I gathered my strength and called Chabane to ask if I should continue with the preparations for the Cabinet meeting that was to be held in two days' time, on Wednesday 2 February. He advised me to do so as he was confident that he would manage to convince Zuma to redeploy me to another position in government.

I left the office just after lunch, worried that I would break down and tell my staff what had transpired. I found myself becoming increasingly upset that Zuma could simply have me removed without following due process. I got home earlier than usual, to the surprise of my wife and my two boys. One of my sons even jokingly asked if I was home so early because I had been fired. I joked back as I did not have the strength to break the news to my family yet.

I went to sleep early and woke up in the early hours of the morning and started going through the Cabinet file. For the rest of the day I anxiously awaited news from Chabane, but the day ended without a call from him and I didn't want to pressure him.

The Cabinet room in the Union Buildings is arranged in a semicircular form, with the outer row of seats for ministers and deputy ministers, and the supporting officials seated in the inner circle. I sat directly in front of Zuma and often had to stand up to pass a note or say something to him or to Collins Chabane.

On the morning of 2 February, I arrived for the Cabinet meeting not knowing what to expect. Zuma was already seated and going through his documents when I got there. I walked over to my seat and greeted him politely. He responded with equal civility but didn't lift his head.

I rushed over to Chabane as soon as he entered the room. I wanted to find out if he had spoken to the president about my situation, but he told me he had not yet managed to secure a meeting. The Cabinet meeting went on as normal until the tea break at 10.30 am. Cellphones weren't allowed in the meeting and had to be left in storage boxes outside. When I collected my phone a flood of text messages lit up the screen. I couldn't open and read a single message without another being received. I wove my way through the group of ministers to get some fresh air and privacy to see what was going on.

I had just reached the outside corridor when I got a call from a member of my team to inform me that e.tv was running a breaking news story that I had been fired. My office wanted to know whether it was true. I was stunned. I told the team member to ignore the calls until I could establish the facts. I looked at my phone again and saw that I had more than 30 missed calls, and still the text messages kept coming.

The next moment I received a call from Hajra Omarjee, a journalist at e.tv, wanting my comment. Omarjee also confided in me that I was apparently to be replaced by Mzwanele 'Jimmy' Manyi, then president of the Black Management Forum. Manyi had been suspended as director-general in the Department of Labour in June the previous year after complaints by the Norwegian ambassador about his conduct during an official meeting.

I decided to stick to my and Chabane's decision not to share the information about my removal from GCIS, and told Omarjee it was not true that I had been fired. This was actually factually correct at the time since Chabane was still exploring the option of a new position for me. After ending the call with Omarjee, I went straight to Chabane to inform him about the leak. Exasperated, he asked me to wait outside the Cabinet room while he tried to speak to the president.

Just as the ministers started walking back into the room, Chabane rushed out and said the president had confirmed that I was no longer CEO of GCIS, and that Manyi had been appointed in my place. I struggled to understand what had just happened. Clearly, Zuma had made the call about my sudden removal and Manyi's appointment without discussing it with Chabane, never mind with me. I could see that Chabane was as disturbed as I was at this development.

I asked Chabane whether I should go back into the Cabinet meeting to continue with preparations for the post-Cabinet media briefing, or leave. He advised me to continue with the meeting and said he would try to come up with a plan to handle the fallout.

I walked back to my seat dejectedly. However, Zuma continued to preside over the meeting as if nothing had happened. The proceedings went on for another two hours or so.

At the end of the meeting, Zuma told the members of Cabinet that Chabane had an announcement to make about some changes in government. Chabane then told the Cabinet meeting that I would be leaving GCIS and this would be my last Cabinet meeting. He also announced that Manyi would be taking over as the new CEO of GCIS and government spokesperson.

Then, to my shock, he announced that I had been redeployed to the position of director-general in the Department of Public Service and Administration. He didn't give any reason for this decision, and the lack of enthusiasm in his voice gave away his uncertainty.

The room went quiet for a few moments. Then the silence was broken by sports minister Fikile Mbalula, who banged the table in a celebratory manner while shouting, 'Yes, yes!' I was not sure whether he was celebrating the news of my departure or Manyi's appointment. Then Zuma stood up and abruptly left the meeting.

I remained in my seat as the meeting adjourned, trying to digest the news of my new position. As I slowly collected my papers, I looked around to see if I could have a quick chat with Richard Baloyi, then minister of public service and administration, and realised he had not actually attended the meeting. A few ministers approached me to offer their commiseration and to thank me for my work as government spokesperson.

I wanted to avoid an awkward situation with the ministers who usually had their lunch just outside the Cabinet room, but then I decided I didn't want anyone to think I was unhappy about my redeployment. So I went outside, looking for Chabane, who asked me to come to his office. I was sad that my team had to learn of my departure through the media and was concerned about the impact it was likely to have on their morale. I also wanted clarity on whether I needed to prepare the post-Cabinet media statement, as I was effectively no longer government spokesperson.

On my way to Chabane's office, I was approached by Mbalula, who uttered what sounded like an apology for his behaviour earlier. We shook hands, and I told him that his conduct had not concerned me at all.

To say that Chabane was disturbed by the turn of events in the Cabinet meeting would be an understatement. He was livid, and he apologised profusely to me. 'I hope you understand that the situation was beyond my control,' he said. He explained that even though he had not had a chance to discuss the matter with Richard Baloyi, he had decided to announce my redeployment in order to avoid a situation in which the government could be accused of unfair labour practice. As he was close to Baloyi and knew the position of director-general in his department was vacant, he felt he would be able to salvage it after the announcement was made. In short, he was forced to think on his feet and to make the call before he could discuss it with me.

We agreed that I would hold my last post-Cabinet media briefing the following day. I didn't have the courage to return to the office and face my staff, so I decided to find a spot in the Union Buildings where I could prepare the Cabinet statement. As I stepped out of his office, the long and often dark corridors looked even darker than usual.

I bumped into Kgalema Motlanthe, who kindly invited me to lunch in his office. The deputy president comforted me and let me know many ministers that had spoken to him after the Cabinet meeting were shocked and disappointed at the decision to remove me. While he did not agree with the president's call, he was powerless to do anything about it, he said. He advised me to take courage and know that I had his full support. He also told me that the majority of ministers believed I had done a great job as head of government communication.

I thanked him for his support. Having that talk with him really saved me that day; I didn't realise how much I needed someone to help me make sense of what had just happened.

That afternoon my phone rang *again* and the name displayed was someone I thought I would never speak to again – Ajay Gupta. I ignored the call but later regretted it. Maybe there was truth in Ajay's threat to have me removed. I realised that a new mode of operation was taking hold in government when the president could show such disregard for the country's labour laws.

I still had to prepare the post-Cabinet media statement, and while I was doing this I got a call from my office informing me that Manyi had

With Phindi and then deputy president, Kgalema Motlanthe (right), at a
pre-lekgotla ministerial dinner at the presidential guest house in Pretoria.

called, wanting to know when he could move into the building to
occupy his office. I was utterly dumbfounded that he wanted to move
in so quickly and that he didn't even bother to call me about a handover, but I told my staff to make the necessary arrangements with him.

After I had drawn up the Cabinet statement, I decided I had better
reach out to Richard Baloyi to let him know that I would be announcing to the media the following day that I was his new director-general.
I didn't want him to hear about it in the media. As could be expected,
Baloyi was stunned when I told him the news, and he expressed his
unhappiness and disbelief that he had not been consulted about the
move. I apologised and advised him to speak to Chabane. However, I
explained that as it had already been announced in the Cabinet meeting, I had no choice but to make a public announcement.

Sadly, my family and friends got to hear about my removal from
GCIS through the media. The first radio reports went out after the

Cabinet meeting and before I could call my wife to inform her about the developments. Phindile called me during the course of the afternoon to find out what was happening, and I was able to soften the blow by telling her that I had been transferred to the Department of Public Service and Administration. I could tell from the tone of her voice and the questions she asked that she suspected something was amiss.

The following day, at the post-Cabinet media briefing, I officially announced my resignation as government spokesperson and thanked the media for their cooperation. 'I think that you are a great crowd – troublesome from time to time, but generally I think you are a great crowd,' I even managed to add jokingly.[18]

Not wanting any rumours to spread or the government to be put in a bad light, I also denied the rumours that had been going around since the previous day that I had been fired because of communication issues around Nelson Mandela's hospitalisation.

My departure from GCIS was so sudden that I never even had the chance to pack my personal belongings, say goodbye to the staff or even do a proper handover to Manyi. In fact, my last time in the office was the Tuesday before the fateful Cabinet meeting. Chabane and the GCIS staff tried to arrange a farewell party for me, but I declined because I simply didn't have the energy and felt it would be best if I tried to settle into my new responsibilities as soon as possible.

I started at the Department of Public Service and Administration about a week after I left GCIS. It took me a few days to finally secure a meeting with Baloyi, at which time he repeated his displeasure that he had not been consulted on my appointment. Baloyi and I had known each other for many years and we respected each other. I never got the sense that his unhappiness had anything to do with me personally, but I could understand his dismay that a new director-general was being forced on him in such a way.

I was quite worried that no official announcement had been made within the department to inform staff that they now had a new director-general, and there was no official welcoming. At least Baloyi introduced me to the staff in his office. I was disappointed to learn early on that the department's leadership was not united, largely due to many years of leadership instability, especially at the director-general level. I also had to assume my position without a letter of appointment or an employment contract.

One of the difficulties I faced was securing meetings with Baloyi. Often, I found myself standing in a queue with other officials outside either his office or his official residence. I also felt that I was not invited to the important meetings that a director-general would ordinarily be part of as the accounting officer of the department. For example, during departmental salary negotiations I was excluded from meetings held with the unions, National Treasury and other departments.

Generally, I felt unwelcome in the department, and I battled with the minister's hands-on approach, which basically left me feeling like an administrative clerk. I also struggled with the fact that senior officials felt more comfortable reporting directly to him than to me. I also got the sense that the management team was divided and that there was much backbiting and mistrust. Much of the tension in the executive team arose from their competition for Baloyi's attention and protection.

I shared my frustrations with Ayanda Dlodlo, then deputy minister in the department. She became a pillar of support. Under normal circumstances I might have been able to deal with the situation, but I found it very demanding, as I was still trying to digest what had happened to me at GCIS. I was emotionally drained, and in June 2011 I came to the conclusion that perhaps the time had come for me to leave the public service. I set up a meeting with Baloyi to inform him that I wanted to explore opportunities in the private sector. Reluctantly, I also told him I wasn't happy with the manner in which I had been treated. While I had received legal advice that the manner in which

I had been removed from GCIS amounted to unfair labour practice, I opted rather to settle with the government.

I officially left the public service at the end of July 2011. I didn't realise how tired I was until after my last day and my final meeting with Baloyi when he told me that Zuma had approved my exit package. I couldn't wait to get in my car and leave not only the department but also Pretoria.

As with my arrival, the staff of the Department of Public Service and Administration learnt about my departure from the media. I was really disappointed that I never managed to blend in and make things work in this department, as I believe it is one of the most important departments in the public service. It has the responsibility of looking after the well-being of all government employees and should lead by example in making sure staff are the first to know about leadership changes in the department. I regret that this never applied to my case.

10

I decide to speak out

After leaving the public service, I spent the next few months trying to get as much rest as possible. I caught up on my reading and played a lot of golf, either alone or with my eldest son, Thabo, who had turned professional in the sport. Emotionally, it was a tough time. I couldn't help but feel discarded and unappreciated, but I also had to accept that life must go on.

To this day, I believe that I did my job to the best of my ability and only in the interests of the country and its citizens. At no stage did I expect this would become a crime under an ANC government. As CEO of GCIS and as government spokesperson, I never tried to undermine Zuma, and I believe I followed the correct procedure with the media conference around Mandela's treatment in hospital.

At the time I didn't understand the full extent of what was happening in the country, in particular what has come to be known as state capture. While I suspected that my refusal to work with the Guptas had helped to seal my fate, I mostly thought I had been caught up in the ANC's factional infighting. The Zuma faction tried to purge Mbeki-ites from key government positions and asserted themselves in an 'it's our time to eat' manner. I was seen to be a Mbeki man.

For a long time, I didn't realise that Zuma and the Guptas had a grand plan to establish an alternative state in which the Guptas would make key decisions, including on the appointment of ministers and key personnel in SOEs and important government departments. My naivety in this regard was exposed on social media in 2012 when, in a tweet, I tried to defend Duduzane Zuma's right to be involved in public-sector-related deals. My view at the time was that the children of politicians should not be prevented from doing business with government. I was severely criticised for this tweet by a number of people and I soon realised that I had not applied my mind to the ethical issues and conflict of interest that this created. It had also not yet dawned on me that the Guptas had not only captured Zuma but were also using his children to access government contracts.

My disappointment was mostly aimed at the ANC for not intervening when I informed them of the Guptas' efforts to channel government resources to their company. I simply trusted that Collins Chabane would raise the matter with his NEC colleagues and that somehow the matter would be resolved. Once again, I was naive to expect Chabane to challenge the party and the head of government. I trusted the political process, and when it failed I accepted my fate.

Although I was angry about the way I had been pushed out of GCIS, my anger was contained. I was under the impression this had only happened to me. However, my anger grew as I became more aware that it wasn't just about pushing out those who were seen as Mbeki supporters but was mostly about efforts at capturing state institutions.

I received a financial settlement when I left government, but I knew I had to move fast to either secure a job in the private sector or start my own business. I tried a few business ventures, but not all of them were successful. These included management and communication consulting, property development, solar energy, converting buses from petrol to gas and the provision of student accommodation. I was part of a company that developed an affordable solar-powered streetlight for townships and informal settlements, but the project never got off the ground because we couldn't get buy-in from any municipalities. I realised that you needed to know someone on the inside before your project could even be considered. After a while, I gave up.

In March 2013 South Africa hosted the fifth summit of the heads of state of Brazil, Russia, India, China and South Africa (BRICS) at the International Convention Centre in Durban. The summit was established to promote economic cooperation among member states by providing financial support for infrastructure and other projects to its members and other developing nations. It was the first time South Africa had hosted the summit.

I was at home on 5 March, the first day of the summit, and decided to watch the live coverage of the proceedings on the SABC's *Morning Live* show. The presenter announced that they would cross to the arrival of the heads of state, who were to be led by Zuma. To my utter amazement, the person walking in front of Zuma and the other leaders was none other than Atul Gupta.

I leant forward to check that I wasn't imagining things. It was unprecedented for a businessperson to precede political leaders at such a high-powered government event involving heads of state. I had been a government employee for long enough to know that this role should have been performed by Maite Nkoana-Mashabane, then minister of international relations and cooperation, the director-general of her department or the government's head of protocol. And yet there was Atul ushering the leaders into the room and extending his hand to direct Zuma to his seat.

At that moment it dawned on me that the Guptas' influence reached far wider than I realised. I started connecting the dots, from my interactions with Ajay Gupta on the IMC, what I had heard about Ajay's role during Zuma's state visit to India, his and his brother Tony's calls to me in 2010 and now this. I realised that the Gupta brothers were slowly usurping state authority and becoming an alternative state.

The BRICS summit was something of an 'aha' moment for me. For the first time I felt anger, because I understood that what had happened to me at GCIS was not an isolated incident. I started to see the bigger picture of what the Guptas were trying to achieve and that our revolution was being sold out to a private family by Zuma.

I sank into my chair, grateful that it was still early in the morning and the only refreshment my wife would allow me to have was a hot cup of coffee. That morning I made the decision that something had to be done: the Guptas had to be stopped. I had no idea how to go about it, but this incremental hijacking of our democracy had to be exposed.

On Tuesday 30 April 2013, senior journalist Barry Bateman reported for Eyewitness News (EWN) that a commercial aircraft carrying wedding guests of the Guptas had landed at Waterkloof Air Force Base in Pretoria. The guests were attending the wedding of the daughter of the Gupta brothers' only sister at Sun City in the Pilanesberg. Police vehicles from the flying squad and VIP protection unit could be seen escorting dozens of white Range Rovers out of the base.[19]

The landing of a commercial aircraft at a military facility and national key point immediately caused an uproar. The same day, even the ANC issued a strongly worded statement in which the party's secretary-general, Gwede Mantashe, objected to how 'guests of a family hosting some wedding at Sun City' could land at a national key point. 'We demand that those who are responsible for granting access to land aircraft in our country also explain the basis upon which such permission was granted, particularly to land at Water-kloof Air Force Base. Those who cannot account must be brought to book,' the statement read.[20]

The incident was covered extensively by the local media and I couldn't help but notice that it caught government communicators off-guard. Journalists were sent from pillar to post, since no one at the South African Air Force, the Department of Defence, the Department of International Relations and Cooperation or the Presidency apparently knew who had authorised the landing at Waterkloof. It was also not clear at the time who had authorised the police escort to Sun City and whether the 200 or so guests had gone through the correct immigration procedures on arrival.

When Bruce Koloane, the chief of state protocol, was fingered as being responsible for the landing, he claimed he had been put under pressure by 'number one', believed to be President Zuma. Years later, Koloane, by then ambassador to the Netherlands, retracted this claim and admitted that he had abused the power of his office to put pressure on defence officials to facilitate the Gupta Waterkloof landing.[21] When Koloane appeared before the Zondo Commission in 2019, he testified that he had used Zuma's name and that of two other ministers to ensure that the defence officials give the necessary clearance.[22] After his testimony, Koloane lost his ambassadorial posting and was recalled to South Africa.

The Waterkloof episode enraged the South African public. The Gupta family had not only undermined the authority of the state but also placed our national security at risk.

Undeterred, in August 2013 the Guptas expanded their media company by starting a 24-hour television station called Africa News Network 7 (ANN7), based in Midrand. Although the channel had state-of-the-art broadcasting equipment, it lacked technical expertise and employed inexperienced presenters who made amateurish errors such as mispronouncing the names of political leaders. What discredited ANN7 more than anything else was its failure to provide balanced reporting and to follow the basic tenets of journalism, such as offering the right of reply to individuals targeted by the channel's reporting and analysis. The ANN7 team introduced relatively unknown 'analysts' who specialised in making unfounded allegations and slandering anyone who criticised the Gupta family.

Over the next three years I became increasingly angry with myself for not doing more to expose what was going on. I also became angry with my party, the ANC, for turning a blind eye to what was happening.

By 2014, most if not all NEC members and ministers either knew or ought to have known that the Guptas were using their friendship with Zuma to gain undue and unlawful influence over the affairs of the state and most, if not all, state entities. Signs that things were going terribly wrong were there for all to see. The most glaring of these were Zuma's inexplicable Cabinet reshuffles, often announced late at night, which saw the promotion of very junior ANC members to key economic portfolios such as finance, energy and mining. Yet, the NEC continued to look the other way.

It was painful to watch Parliament and its committees being turned into defence committees for Zuma and state capture. I found it hard to contain my anger, and I started turning to Twitter to voice my disappointment and anger. This contributed to my being perceived as an enemy of the revolution. When my father passed away in December 2014, I couldn't help but notice that many people I thought would come to support me and my family did not attend the funeral. I retreated from many of the business consortia that I was invited to join because I suspected that my name was becoming a stumbling block, or a curse, to these groups. I became aware of numerous examples of individuals who had been 'blacklisted', not necessarily for whistleblowing but for being perceived as part of the Mbeki faction. In his book *Eight Days in September*, Frank Chikane tellingly writes about how he was blocked from getting a job for exactly this reason: '. . . I was either blocked from existing business interests, including opportunities for employment, or business was made to understand that I was a *persona non grata* and that they should have nothing to do with me. This also closed opportunities to serve on the boards of private companies.'[23] Indeed, I came to realise that being on the wrong side not just of the ruling party but of a dominant faction within the ruling party could lead to diminished opportunities because, despite their public utterances, businesses tend to want to be in the good books of politicians. This could be out of fear that employing someone who is disliked by a particular faction could limit their chances of winning a government tender or that the dominant faction could swing government policy to the detriment of a business of a whole sector. In fact, at ANC fundraising events, Zuma was never shy of making the point that those businesses who support the ANC will do well. At a fundraising dinner to celebrate the ANC's 101st birthday, he was quoted as saying, 'Everything you touch will multiply. I've always said that a wise businessperson will support the ANC . . . because supporting the ANC means you're investing very well in your business.'[24]

On 16 March 2016 Deputy Minister of Finance Mcebisi Jonas released a statement through the finance ministry confirming that, the previous year, the Gupta family had offered him the position of finance minister. They told him that then finance minister Nhlanhla Nene was going to be fired and offered him a R600 million bribe to work with them.[25]

Following Jonas's statement, the *Financial Times* reported that a contact had made a claim to the newspaper that the Guptas had offered Jonas the position, which the Guptas denied.[26] That Sunday the *Sunday Times* carried a story under the headline 'How Guptas shopped for new minister', which said that President Jacob Zuma's son Duduzane had been present when members of the Gupta family had offered Jonas the job of finance minister.[27]

According to Jonas's statement, he had rejected the offer: 'The basis of my rejection of their offer is that it makes a mockery of our hard-earned democracy, the trust of our people and no one apart from the president of the republic appoints ministers.'[28]

Two days before Jonas's statement, Vytjie Mentor, a former ANC MP who had chaired the portfolio committee on public enterprises, alleged in a Facebook post that the Gupta brothers had offered her the position of minister of public enterprises in late 2010, claiming that the incumbent minister, Barbara Hogan, would be replaced soon.[29] The offer was made on condition that Mentor ensured that SAA dropped their Johannesburg-to-Mumbai route so that India's Jet Airways could acquire it. She further alleged that President Zuma was at the Gupta residence in Saxonwold when these discussions took place.

About a month earlier, Julius Malema, by then the leader of the Economic Freedom Fighters (EFF), claimed that in 2010 Fikile Mbalula, who was deputy minister of police at the time, had been offered the position of sports minister by the Guptas.[30] Initially, Mbalula denied these allegations and insisted that he had been appointed by Zuma. (It transpired later that Mbalula had received a call from Ajay Gupta before his appointment as sports minister was announced, to congratulate him on what would be his new position. In 2011 Mbalula informed a meeting of the NEC about the call.)

It had been five years since I had left the civil service, and with each passing year the influence of the Gupta family in the affairs of state became increasingly clear. After the Waterkloof landing they became a regular feature in news reports and the term 'state capture' entered the South African lexicon. A number of civil society organisations, such as the South African Council of Churches, and political parties began to speak out about the Guptas' political influence and the lucrative business deals they were striking with state institutions thanks to their friendship with Zuma.

I was deeply saddened and concerned by the inaction of the ANC leadership and the government on the matter, which was looking more and more like an informal coup d'état. For months, I had pondered speaking out about my own experiences, and Jonas's statement was just the catalyst I needed.

I had not yet made up my mind who to approach when I was contacted by the journalist Moshoeshoe Monare, whom I had known since my days as head of education in Gauteng, when he was an education reporter for *The Star*. Over the years, Moshoeshoe had become a friend and I had told him about my meeting with the Guptas in 2010. He had tried to convince me many times before to do a media interview and speak out in public about my experiences with the family, but I always wavered, mainly because I thought mine had been an isolated incident.

About a day after Jonas's media statement, Moshoeshoe called me to say it was now or never. He caught me at just the right time – finally, I was ready to talk. The only snag was that he was no longer working as part of the editorial team but was in a managerial position at the Times Media Group, which owned the *Sunday Times*. I agreed to do the interview for the *Sunday Times* on condition that Moshoeshoe did the interview and then briefed trusted journalists to write up the story.

That Saturday morning I went for my regular 15-kilometre run – more than ever before I needed to clear my head. Even though I had agreed to meet Moshoeshoe at 11 am, I still had doubts about whether or not to proceed with the interview, because I realised what the potential impact would be. I expected many people would be unhappy with me for exposing Zuma in such a way, and for causing harm to the ANC, which was also still my political home.

Moshoeshoe was 15 minutes early and arrived with a mischievous smile, as if to say, 'You finally agreed to do it.' I offered him coffee – or something stronger – but he declined. He didn't realise that I was in effect offering myself the drink because I desperately needed it.

I grabbed two chairs and we went to sit outside, out of earshot. I didn't want my wife to hear the details of the interview. I had told her that I would be interviewed by a journalist but didn't say what it was about. I suspected she might try to dissuade me from going ahead due to the controversy it was likely to generate.

'Hey, monna, let's talk,' Moshoeshoe said, wasting no time.

'Where do you want me to start?' I asked.

'From the beginning.'

I told him about that first call from Ajay Gupta requesting a meeting and the call from Zuma asking me to help the Gupta brothers on the day of my meeting with Ajay. I also described what had happened at the meeting in Saxonwold and my refusal to transfer the GCIS budget to the Gupta media empire. Then there were the calls from Tony and Ajay Gupta a few months later demanding a meeting while I was on my way to Sun City. I also told Moshoeshoe about my unlawful removal as GCIS CEO and government spokesperson.

In between he asked many probing questions. The interview – all on the record – concluded about two hours later with a request from Moshoeshoe that I keep my phone switched on as one of his journalists might call with further questions. He also informed me that they would call some of the people I had named to get their comments. I expected a few of my journalist friends would be unhappy that I had not given them the story, but it was a matter of Moshoeshoe being at the right place at the right time.

After Moshoeshoe left, my wife was naturally curious to know more about the interview, especially as it had taken so long. She could tell that I was not myself and was a little anxious. I told her that the interview was about my experiences with the Guptas after Zuma asked me to help them, and that the reason it had taken so long was because of all the questions Moshoeshoe had asked. Naturally, she was a bit concerned. She realised that the article would likely draw a lot of media interest and she worried about my being exposed.

The rest of the day dragged by, and that night I only slept for about three hours. A nearby petrol station always received its stock of Sunday newspapers earlier than other shops. By 5 am I was there to buy a copy of the *Sunday Times*, but, as fate would have it, the delivery was late that morning. I drove to another petrol station but they also didn't have any newspapers yet. I was still driving around when I saw a guy putting up a poster on a street pole screaming something like 'Government official spills the beans'. Now I was even more desperate to get hold of a copy.

I drove back to the petrol station near our house at about 6.30am and saw a delivery van offloading newspapers. When I entered the shop, a man was standing in front of the newspaper shelf, reading the paper and blocking my way. He was so engrossed that I had to clear my throat to make him aware that I also wanted a copy. He immediately picked up the *Sunday Times* and stood aside. As he moved aside, he looked at his paper, then stared at me before looking down at his paper again.

I smiled, unsure of why he was acting so strangely, but then I finally got sight of the front page – my face was splashed across it. The headline read 'Zuma told me to help Guptas'.[31] The brother had recognised me, and then of course he asked whether it was indeed me on the front page.

'No, that's my twin brother,' I said lightheartedly. He instantly got the joke and winked at me.

When I went to pay, I discovered that I'd forgotten my wallet at home, but thankfully the cashier knew me as a regular customer and told me to take a copy and come back later to pay. I grabbed the *Sunday Times* and drove to a quiet spot where I first just stared at the newspaper. I knew the story was likely to be big and controversial, but I didn't expect it to be on the front page. In that moment I also realised that the proverbial shit was now definitely going to hit the fan. I panicked, since I had done something that was taboo in ANC politics: I had snitched on the president and on my party.

I drove home as fast as I could, knowing that life as I knew it was about to change. By the time I got there, Phindile had already left for church, but she read the article the moment she got back. As she read, she tried to hide her emotions but I could see she was shocked by the prominence given to the article. While I had informed her that I would be doing the interview with Moshoeshoe, I felt guilty that I had not first discussed my going public with her, as her life would also be impacted by the article.

The first media call came around eight and my phone did not stop ringing thereafter. I must have done more than 30 radio interviews by lunch time, and I also received several calls from family and friends congratulating me for 'coming out' and offering their support. Although I didn't expect the overwhelming encouragement from family and friends, I welcomed it with open arms. One of the calls came from Sydney Mufamadi, my political mentor and a close family friend, and his younger brother, Vhonani, who also offered their support. Sydney drew my attention to another report in the newspaper about a statement issued by a group of ANC stalwarts condemning the undue influence of the Gupta family on matters of the state and the ANC's failure to address the malaise. Bra Syd's call and the report about the ANC stalwarts went a long way towards making me feel less alone and reducing my stress levels.

That afternoon I was inundated with further requests for radio and television interviews. I sorely missed the infrastructure I had when I was still at GCIS. Here I was, the former government spokesperson, with no media strategy to handle an unfolding story, due to my failure to anticipate the media and public interest it would generate. I was swamped. At least I had the support of my wife, who stood by me through that day and over the following weeks as I became one of the faces associated with exposing state capture by the Gupta family.

For the first time in my life, I regretted the decision not to change my mobile telephone number when I left GCIS. I started receiving strange and threatening calls from strangers. One caller told me I should never dare set foot in KwaZulu-Natal ever again. Several police and private security assessments considered the threat levels serious enough to advise me to not travel to the province even though

Durban was my favourite holiday destination. Some of the changes I had to implement as part of the security precautions included avoiding large gatherings, never driving on the same route, driving past my house at least twice before driving in, always sitting with my back to the wall in public places such as restaurants and never parking in the same spot in public parking lots.

Over the next few days I realised that the one thing I hadn't factored in when I decided to speak out was the impact it would have on my family. For instance, one of my sons was friends with one of Zuma's sons, and the other was a friend and classmate of the son of one of the Gupta brothers. While my son's friendship with the Zuma boy was not affected by the *Sunday Times* article, the relationship between my other son and the Gupta boy fizzled out. In hindsight, I should have alerted my boys to the fact that I was going to be in the media and would be implicating their friends' parents in wrongdoing.

Speaking out will often have an impact on those you love and care about. Spouses and children have their own circles of relationships and lives that can be heavily affected by your actions. The least you should do is take them into your confidence and let them know what you are about to do, to prepare them for how your actions may affect them.

Obviously, your family could advise you against becoming a whistleblower, but that is a choice every individual needs to take on their own. At the time, I made my decision based on something I once heard Nelson Mandela say, that fools multiply when wise men are silent. I felt the country would not be best served if I remained silent simply out of family considerations.

The *Sunday Times* article put me in the spotlight in ways I never could have anticipated. One positive result was that I received requests for interviews from local and international media houses, and I want to believe that my speaking out offered further proof of the Guptas' role in state capture and helped to put pressure on both them and Zuma.

At the same time, I began to experience ostracism from many in the ANC. Although many ANC leaders and comrades were very supportive in private, not many were willing to support me in public. Some seemed unsure of how to handle their relationship with me. They would praise me and give a comradely hug in private with a whispered 'Well done,' 'I wish I was as brave as you' or 'We are with you, comrade,' but a mere wave would suffice at public gatherings such as political meetings or funerals.

I realised that some did not want to be seen to be associating with anyone perceived to have snitched on one of their own. I was on the receiving end of a double whammy because I was perceived by some to be part of the Mbeki faction and by others to be a snitch. After the *Sunday Times* article I realised that my phone was not ringing as often as it used to. In fact, there were times when I thought my line had been disconnected. My calls were also not returned as quickly as they used to be, both by those in government who I thought supported me and by others in business circles, and were sometimes not answered at all. It became increasingly difficult to secure meetings.

I was taken by surprise when I heard that the matter of the Guptas would be discussed at the NEC meeting scheduled for the end of March 2016. Up to that point, the ANC had seemed unwilling to deal with the issue, since nearly half of the NEC members were staunch Zuma supporters.

At the meeting, the NEC mandated the office of the secretary-general to investigate the influence of the Guptas on government and Cabinet appointments. At a media briefing, secretary-general Gwede Mantashe repeatedly stated that the ANC had full confidence in President Zuma, but he also invited ANC members and members of the public to come forward and provide information about the Guptas to his office. Mantashe also said that those who made statements to the party would not face repercussions and would be politically protected.[32]

I listened to Mantashe with mixed emotions. While I was pleased that the matter was receiving attention at the highest level within the party, I was sceptical at how good the ANC would be at investigating itself. I was struck by Mantashe's statement that people who spoke out would be politically protected and that no action would be taken against them. I decided there and then that I would accept the invitation to give information about my experiences with the Guptas.

I called Mantashe a few days later to inform him that I was willing to come forward, and a meeting was arranged for a few days later. The meeting was scheduled for 6 pm at Luthuli House, but I arrived early to give myself enough time to prepare and also to calm myself. When I got to the reception area, I realised that I had not been there for more than two years and barely recognised any of the staff members who were going in and out of the building.

Mantashe kicked off the meeting by thanking me for making time to meet him and for being brave enough to accept the NEC invitation. I knew Mantashe from meetings and activities during the struggle when he was secretary-general of the National Union of Mineworkers. I have always found him a very likeable person who enjoys a good laugh, so it was no surprise when he shared a few jokes about 'ama-gwala akwa-ANC' (ANC cowards) who were too scared to speak out about Zuma and the Guptas.

He then invited me to share my experiences with the Guptas and my interaction with Zuma around the family. I was very impressed that he listened to every word I said and also took notes. After I had told him everything, he expressed his shock at what I had shared and asked a few questions.

'Would you be willing to put everything you've said in writing?' he asked.

'Yes, of course.'

'Do not be afraid to share all the information you have given me today,' he said. 'I have been approached by a number of Cabinet ministers and ANC NEC members who expressed their willingness to come forward and make submissions.'

Mantashe did not hold back in sharing his own frustration with the Guptas' alleged influence on Zuma, and he told me that he was committed to leading the fight against any forces that were trying to capture the state or the ANC. He also expressed his concerns about the serious allegations made by Mcebisi Jonas, Fikile Mbalula and Barbara Hogan, the former minister of public enterprises, who had been axed in 2010 and had since come out to say that she had been fired because she refused to cancel the SAA route to Mumbai, India. 'If these allegations are found to be true, it comes down to treason, and the ANC cannot just sit quietly and do nothing,' he said.

I left the meeting feeling very positive and encouraged. I told a few close friends about it, but they were all quite sceptical and thought I was naive to believe that anything would come from this ANC investigation. I defended my decision to participate, saying that the country desperately needed a political solution to the state capture saga. Only the ANC could provide the required leadership, since its president was at the centre of the allegations.

I immediately started working on my written submission and finished it within the week. When I called Mantashe, he suggested I hand it over in person. He was pleased that I had kept my promise to supply a written submission, but I was surprised to hear that no one else had yet made a submission to his office.

After that meeting, I did not hear from Mantashe again until he issued a media statement at the end of May to say the ANC had stopped its investigation into the Guptas and state capture. According to news reports, he said it would be a 'fruitless exercise' to continue, since only one written submission had been received after eight people had originally approached him with complaints about state capture.[33] While Mantashe said that the allegations were serious and could not be treated lightly, and that 'many warrant a comprehensive investigation', I was disappointed in the ANC leadership for their failure to immediately tackle what was becoming one of the biggest scandals of our new democracy.[34]

I felt betrayed, and wondered what had happened to my report. Was it filed in the bottom drawer, shared within the party or perhaps even passed on to the Guptas? I also wondered whether I should be concerned for my personal safety.

Mantashe had not identified the person who made the written submission, which led to speculation in the media about that person's identity. Ray Hartley, a former comrade of mine in the student movement and then editor of *The Times* newspaper, was one of the first journalists to report that I was the only person who had made a submission to the ANC.

After my written submission, my unpopularity in certain ANC circles increased by a factor of 100. Invitations to social gatherings such as soccer or golf games dried up because no person, department or company wanted to be seen to be associated with a whistleblower. I understood why ANC members had difficulty associating with me: they didn't want Zuma, who was both president of the ruling party and president of the country, to hear stories that they had been seen with me. Zuma was very powerful and I had become the enemy of both the state and the party.

I started receiving calls from private numbers where the person on the other end of the line would call me a snitch and never identify himself. I also endured numerous insults and threats from Zuma supporters on Twitter, which I either ignored or simply deleted. During this time I really started to worry about my security and that of my family.

Over the preceding weeks ANN7 had had a field day trying to discredit people like me, Jonas and Mentor. Our faces dominated their broadcasts for days at a time. I recall one programme in which so-called analysts spent the whole show calling the three of us liars.

While there was good reason for me to take legal action, I simply didn't have the financial resources or the mental energy to do so.

I slowly withdrew from public life and entered a phase of self-imposed isolation. I socialised less and steered clear of public events to avoid putting friends or acquaintances in a difficult position. But this gave me the opportunity to spend more time with my wife and sons and the broader extended family. I started attending more family gatherings, such as funerals and weddings, but it wasn't easy, and I realised that I had long delegated these functions to my father (when he was still alive), my wife and my brothers because of my hectic work schedule. Although my sudden reappearance at these family gatherings was welcomed, it wasn't easy for me. I had become quite introverted, while my family still expected the same person they had seen in the newspapers, on television and had listened to on radio for so many years. But I always put on a brave face and never shared the financial and security load I was carrying. I also had to be cautious and always look over my shoulder, especially when I travelled to family events outside Johannesburg.

From 2016 I started experiencing serious financial difficulties as I continued to struggle to find employment. The banks were starting to call in loans I had taken out. My attempts to find a job in the private sector drew a blank. I tried to reach out to businesspeople I knew, but my CV seemed to end up on the bottom shelf as I never made it past 'acknowledgement of receipt'. John Dludlu, a friend and former editor of the *Sowetan*, tried to submit my name to a number of SOEs and private companies, including for board appointments, but without any results. At one point I told Dludlu he should stop trying, since I had clearly become an 'untouchable' in both the public and the private sectors.

Needless to say, I also couldn't raise funding for further business initiatives because I was considered a business risk.

While I have never regretted my decision to make a submission to the ANC, in retrospect I might have been naive to expect that something would come from an investigation that originated with an NEC dominated by Zuma supporters. However, while the NEC's decision to investigate the matter did not lead to anything concrete, it did signal that the tide was slowly starting to turn inside the ANC and that pressure was mounting on Zuma.

During this time I also received a call from Bishop Malusi Mpumlwana, the general secretary of the South African Council of Churches, requesting a short meeting to discuss the issue of state capture. In the end we talked for more than two hours, during which time he told me that church leaders supported me for speaking out and were very concerned about the reports of state capture and its impact on poor communities. He said they were preparing a statement on the matter that would be shared with their church members and the general public, and he invited me to make a written submission, whereupon I sent him a copy of the document I had submitted to Gwede Mantashe. Unfortunately, I did not have the time to participate fully in their initiative although I did attend a few of their gatherings.

On 16 May a group of 27 former directors-general who had served in government since 1994, including me, Sipho Pityana, Gibson Njenje, Vusi Pikoli and the Reverend Frank Chikane, released a statement (see Annexure) calling for an independent inquiry into state capture.[35] 'As former DGs,' the statement read, 'we are concerned about reports that public officials, including heads of state-owned entities, are being pressurised by private interests to wilfully break procurement rules and the rules pertaining to transparent, fair and competency-based appointments. In particular, we express concern at recent revelations of "state capture" by the Gupta family, their apparent influence over political and administrative appointments and their alleged involvement in the irregular facilitation, securing and issuing of government tenders and contracts.'[36]

After the release of this statement, my phone started ringing again and I did a few radio and television interviews. For some people, this cemented the view that I was an 'enemy of the state'. What carried me through was the support I received from my family, friends and some members of the public, as well as the belief that I was on the right side of history.

11

The Public Protector calls

For some years the Guptas' newspaper *The New Age* and the ANN7 television station seemed to receive unchecked advertising spend from the public sector, including from SOEs, despite their failure to adhere to basic journalistic standards and no demonstrable audience.

However, in 2016 pressure started to mount on the Gupta media companies. In March the ANC condemned ANN7 and *The New Age* for their reports of an alleged plot by senior ANC members to topple President Jacob Zuma. The NEC described the reporting as 'reckless' and disrespectful. Zizi Kodwa, ANC spokesperson at the time, said the ANC leadership had met with Infinity Media, the holding company for the Guptas' media interests, about the matter and the company had agreed to issue an apology to the ANC for erroneous reporting.[37]

The New Age also became controversial for organising what were called business breakfast briefings with Cabinet ministers, which were broadcast live by the SABC. According to one report, the Department of Communications spent nearly R1 million on a single breakfast session in May 2016.[38] The costs were carried by SOEs such as Eskom, and the SABC carried the live broadcast costs and forfeited all possible advertising revenue that it would have received during normal programming.

Although ANN7 had the potential to provide an alternative voice in the media landscape, it was discredited by its failure to embrace globally accepted journalistic standards, such as the right of reply, separating news from opinion and verifying sources, and by its failure to deliver balanced and professional news to its viewers. Instead, the channel invested a lot of time and resources in projecting Zuma in a positive light, defending him against his detractors and using analysts to attack people like Mentor, Jonas and me. Our faces were splashed on the ANN7 screen on most evenings with no right of reply given to us.

In 2016 a number of ANN7 journalists and anchors demonstrated outside the offices of the station complaining about ill-treatment by the station management and the Gupta brothers. When some staff members protested against an earlier dismissal of eight of their colleagues and refused to attend a staff meeting that was to be addressed by Collen Maine, the president of the ANC Youth League, five journalists were fired and several more received warnings.[39]

After the *Sunday Times* report and my submission to the ANC NEC, I was frequently stopped in shopping malls and on the streets of Johannesburg by people who recognised me. Most of these encounters were with strangers who simply wanted to shake my hand and thank me for speaking out. Encounters like these gave me hope and the courage to continue speaking out, despite the risks involved. However, in a few cases strangers stopped me to ask whether I was 'the Gupta guy' (who was responsible for stealing public funds) because they associated my face with the state capture reports. Knowing these were simply instances of mistaken identity, I could laugh it off.

Then one day I received a call from the office of Advocate Thuli Madonsela, the Public Protector, requesting an interview with me about my claims around state capture. After Mcebisi Jonas and Vytjie Mentor made public statements that the Guptas had offered them

ministerial positions, the Public Protector received a number of official complaints about the 'alleged improper and unethical conduct
relating to the appointment of Cabinet ministers', the awarding of
state contracts to Gupta-linked companies and the alleged unethical
and improper conduct by the president, and so she instituted an
investigation.[40]

While Madonsela had a reputation for speaking truth to those in
power, I was still a little sceptical whether a state-funded institution
would have the will and capacity to investigate this matter properly.
Yet, I agreed to be interviewed, and asked whether I would need legal
representation. Since I didn't have full-time employment at the time,
I didn't have the resources to get an attorney to accompany me, but
thankfully I was assured it wouldn't be necessary.

I found myself rather anxious in the days leading up to the meeting
with the Public Protector because I didn't know what to expect or how
to prepare. A few friends in the legal fraternity advised that I should
just remember to state the words 'without prejudice' right at the
beginning of the meeting just in case my submission ended up in
court. The night before the meeting, I couldn't fall asleep and contem-
plated postponing it, but after many restless hours I decided to tell
my story without any fear.

Feeling extremely tired from lack of sleep, I had to drag myself to
the meeting, which was to be held at my office in Rosebank. I was
under the impression that the indefatigable Madonsela would conduct
the meeting herself, and I was both disappointed and relieved when
I was told she was held up and that her team would conduct the
interview. After the introductions, I was asked to take an oath. As I
had never before been exposed to these kinds of proceedings, for a
moment I felt rather intimidated by the formality of it all and wondered whether it had been a mistake not to bring legal representation.
At what point do I say 'without prejudice', I wondered. My mind was
put at ease when the team explained that it was a legal requirement

to make my statement under oath. They informed me that they would also be recording the interview and that I could get a copy of the recording. In the end, I never even got round to saying 'without prejudice'!

The interview was scheduled to be two hours' long but went on for about three. It was a relief to finally be done. The interview made me realise that there was no turning back on this road I had set out on, and I could not shy away from further actions required of me, even if it meant going public again. For the time being, I would have to give up my hope of disappearing from the public eye.

The Public Protector's investigation continued for many months. Since her term was due to end on 14 October 2016, there was considerable speculation in the media about whether she would be able to conclude the investigation and finalise her report in time. The determined Madonsela pushed on, and by mid-October she was ready to release her report, simply titled 'State of Capture'. In *No Longer Whispering to Power*, a biography of Madonsela by journalist Thandeka Gqubule, the former Public Protector admits that she deliberately suggested that the Chief Justice should recommend a judge to chair the proposed judicial inquiry into state capture in order to ensure that no one could stop the implementation of the report's findings and recommendations.[41]

Zuma lodged an urgent application to interdict the report, saying that he had not been given an opportunity to respond to questions posed by Madonsela on his relationship with the Guptas, and that he wanted time to interview the witnesses she had spoken to. It was suspected at the time that Zuma wanted to delay the finalisation of the report in the hope that Madonsela's successor would be more sympathetic to him.

Zuma's interdict application was set to be heard at the Pretoria High Court on 1 November. However, on that day Zuma's legal team informed the court that they were withdrawing the application. The court ordered not only that Madonsela's report be released immediately but also that Zuma be held personally liable for the legal costs.

One of the Public Protector's key recommendations in 'State of Capture' was that the president should appoint a judicial commission of inquiry to properly investigate the claims of state capture within 30 days of the release of the report because her office didn't have the necessary resources to conduct a proper investigation. Madonsela further recommended that the commission be headed by a judge, to be selected by the Chief Justice. Madonsela argued that even though the Constitution empowers the president to appoint a judicial commissions of inquiry, this would not be practical since he was an implicated party in the report. Furthermore, the commission should use the 'State of Capture' report as its starting point.

After the release of the Public Protector's report, I felt a huge sense of relief and also some vindication. At least one state agency had taken the allegations around the Guptas very seriously, and I was hopeful that perhaps something might be done to hold the implicated parties accountable.

However, my anxiety levels also rose because I realised I would remain in the public eye for a while longer.

As could be expected, Zuma went on a public offensive against the Public Protector's report and even went to Parliament to defend his friendship with the G-Force, as the Guptas had become known. In December 2016 he took the remedial action recommended by the report on review. This meant that the court would be asked whether the Public Protector had acted in accordance with her powers and whether any aspect of the report was irrational.[42] Zuma wanted the court to review and set aside three of the remedial actions recommended in the report – all three relating to the commission of inquiry he had been asked to set up.

In early 2017 public resentment against Zuma seemed to boil over as the Guptas continued to do business with government and he steadfastly refused to implement the Public Protector's remedial actions.

On 7 April, large demonstrations were held across the country to demand that Zuma should step down. These demonstrations followed yet another Cabinet reshuffle by the president. Social media went wild as protesters posted video clips of people hoisting the South African flag and singing the national anthem. It reminded me of our marches under the banner of the UDF during the struggle years, except this time around the ANC had been caught with its pants down as its unpopular president was under siege. However, some credit should be given to Zuma for finally uniting South Africans of all races, ages and genders.

Although no formal stayaway from work was declared, many South Africans saw fit to take time off from their workplaces, universities and schools to voice their anger at and rejection of the president's actions. Even labour unions and captains of industry joined the protests under the banner of organisations such as Business Unity South Africa and Business Leadership South Africa (BLSA).

Then, in May, something unexpected happened. ANC secretary-general Gwede Mantashe announced that the NEC had decided to support the call for the establishment of a commission of inquiry to investigate the allegations of state capture and the influence of business on the state.[43] Mantashe announced that the NEC called on all individuals, including the president and the opposition parties who had opposed Zuma's review application, not to use the review process in court as a way of slowing down the process of establishing the commission of inquiry.

Then he announced that the inquiry should date back to 1994, 'to look into all other possible cases that had not been investigated by the Public Protector since the ANC came to power'.[44] I nearly fell off my chair when I heard this, as it meant the ANC as a political party was under the impression it could extend the mandate of a judicial inquiry. Mantashe also said: 'If I'm captured by someone other than the Guptas, I'm not better off than people who were captured by the

Guptas . . . that's why we say let's drill deeper to understand the extent of the influence of business on the ANC.'[45]

This signalled to me that the Zuma supporters in the ANC had won the day and had forced the party to make this nonsensical and, in essence, illegal recommendation. It was clear that the ANC had not learnt from the Constitutional Court decision on the Nkandla matter, handed down in March 2016, that any remedial action proposed by the Public Protector was binding and could only be reviewed by a court, not by any other body – including Parliament and political parties.[46]

Once again, the NEC had failed to seize the moment and listen to the voices inside and outside the party who were calling on it to do the right thing and appoint the commission. The NEC wanted to be seen to comply with the Public Protector's remedial actions while appeasing Zuma's supporters in the party. It would be another seven months before the ANC finally took a firm policy position on the implementation of the Public Protector's recommendations.

By June 2017, I was still unemployed and really struggling to make ends meet. One day, I got a call from Bonang Mohale, the chief executive of BLSA, requesting an urgent meeting with me. Bonang, who was a keen supporter of student politics, and I had known each other since our days as students at Wits University and fellow residents of Glen Thomas House. On the day of our meeting, he told me he was in the process of setting up a new executive team at BLSA and offered me the position of director of communications.

I was elated at the job opportunity, but I was nervous that some at BLSA might be concerned about the stigma attached to my name. I asked whether he thought my actions as a whistleblower the previous year presented any reputational concerns for his board. I was incredibly relieved when he said the board would be pleased to be associated with a person of my calibre and that my speaking out against state capture was the very reason why he thought I was the right person to join his organisation. I accepted the job offer on condition that it would be a one-year contract.

To my surprise, he called me a few days later to inform me that I had been appointed. I had anticipated being interviewed by other members of the board.

'When do you want to start?' he asked.

I desperately needed the income and gladly accepted the offer of a one-year contract. In July 2017 I started work as the communications director at BLSA.

In December 2017 the North Gauteng High Court in Pretoria finally gave its ruling in Zuma's review application. That day, a number of civil society organisations, under the banner of Save South Africa, converged on the Pretoria city centre to protest against corruption and state capture. This large and peaceful protest again brought together South Africans from many different walks of life.

The Pretoria march culminated in a public meeting at the Methodist church in the Pretoria city centre, which was addressed by leaders of participating civil society organisations and various church and community leaders. I attended the march and the public meeting in Pretoria as part of the business delegation that was there to support the call for Zuma to step down. I was wearing a white T-shirt with 'SAVE SA' boldly printed on the front.

When I arrived at the church after the march, I was ushered into what the organisers called the VIP holding room outside the main venue, where a number of politicians and CEOs were being served coffee before the start of the public meeting. I felt a bit uncomfortable standing in this room with all these important businesspeople and couldn't wait to join the masses in the hall.

I turned down a number of requests for media interviews, since I was there as a BLSA representative and was worried that I might end up giving my own strong personal views on corruption instead of those of the organisation. So I sneaked out of the VIP section and went into the main hall of the church, which was filled to capacity with people singing at the tops of their voices. The absence of any government ministers or ANC leaders was noticeable, even though a number of ANC members and government officials were present.

My plan was to sit at the back and observe the proceedings from there, but one of the marshals at the door grabbed me by the arm and directed me to the front of the hall, and I ended up sitting in the front row with all the other dignitaries who were already in attendance. Some of the organisers tried to convince me to say a few words to the gathering, but I politely declined. The speakers at the event included retired Justice of the Constitutional Court Zak Yacoob, Save South Africa founder and leader Sipho Pityana and a host of other religious and civil society leaders.

The court's ruling was made while the public meeting was in session. When the MC announced that the court proceedings in the *Zuma v Public Protector* case had been concluded, everyone rose to their feet in anticipation. You could cut the tense atmosphere in the room with a knife. Then the MC announced that Zuma's application to review and set aside the remedial actions of the Public Protector's report was dismissed. The court also ordered that Zuma should appoint a commission of inquiry within 30 days and 'take all steps, do all things and sign all documents which are necessary to give effect to the remedial action'.

In addition, the court ordered Zuma to pay the costs of his review application in his personal capacity.[47] A number of opposition parties, including the EFF, UDM and COPE, specifically took issue with the president's use of the State Attorney to represent him in the matter. According to the court ruling, these parties made the point that 'in his alleged dealings with the Gupta family, he was not acting in his official capacity as the President of the country and Member of the National Executive'.[48]

In his ruling, Judge President Dunstan Mlambo said that the Public Protector's report had uncovered 'worrying levels of malfeasance and corruption in the form of utter disregard of good corporate governance principles, some bordering on fraud, in government departments and SOEs. This invariably involves large amounts of taxpayer funds and state resources . . . In our view the President had no justifiable basis to simply ignore the impact of this corruption on the South African public. His conduct also falls far short of the expectation on him as Head of State to support institutions of democracy such as the Public Protector. The remedial action of the Public Protector presented him with an opportunity to confront and address the problem.'[49]

I still vividly recall the jubilation, wild singing and dancing that took place inside the Methodist church when the court's decision was announced. In fact, the gathering turned into one of the biggest celebrations I have ever experienced since FW de Klerk's announcement that Mandela would be released and the announcement that South Africa would host the 2010 FIFA World Cup.

I could not hold back the tears. I covered my face and sobbed quietly as I tried to take everything in. Even though I felt overjoyed, there was also a sense of sadness. This kind of internal turmoil had become the new normal for me in the preceding years. Here I was, a former struggle activist who was participating in a historic gathering where a court decision *against* the president of my government and of my party, the ANC, was being celebrated. Zuma had been found by the court to have acted in a manner that undermined not only the rule of law but also the values that underpinned the democratic constitution that we had fought for decades to create.

Then one of my comrades came over and grabbed my hand, dragging me to the centre of the church, where the large crowd was dancing. I didn't hold back at all and I joined the celebratory dancing and singing, hugging everyone around me. I celebrated the court decision because I knew that our democracy had come close to the brink of being destroyed by the G-Force and their partners in the looting brigade.

In December 2017 the ANC's long-awaited 54th national conference took place at the National Sports and Recreation Exhibition Centre (Nasrec) in the south of Johannesburg. I attended as part of the BLSA delegation. I wanted to be there to witness how the Zuma and Ramaphosa factions would battle it out for the party leadership, and to hear how they planned to address the challenges facing the party and, most importantly, the nation.

The mood at the conference reminded me of the 2007 Polokwane conference where Zuma defeated Mbeki in the election for the party presidency. It would be the understatement of the century to say the atmosphere was tense and acrimonious. In fact, it was as if it was a conference of two opposing parties. The delegates were intolerant of each other's views and the singing was as factional as at Polokwane.

As was always the case at national conferences, the delegates were seated in different provincial blocs, which further encouraged factional singing. Delegates seldom sang the same songs. Rather, delegates from different provinces sang songs in support of either Cyril Ramaphosa or Nkosazana Dlamini-Zuma, the two leading candidates for the party leadership. After the Polokwane conference, this was the second most embarrassing experience I have endured as an ANC member, as this divisive behaviour was broadcast live on various television and radio stations for all to see and hear.

In an attempt to limit the negative media coverage and limit the risk of stories leaking to the media, the conference organisers had decided to erect a fence around the venue to physically keep journalists away from the conference and its delegates during the closed sessions. It was a little amusing but mostly just sad to see the journalists watching the conference venue from behind the fence. There were reports of journalists being physically pushed away from the Nasrec grounds and into the fenced area.

Journalists were only invited into the venue during open sessions and regular media briefings convened by the ANC leadership. Although I accept that every party is entitled to determine which of its sessions will be open to the media, I thought there were more established and dignified ways of managing the media. The fence created the impression that the ANC saw the media as the enemy, and probably also contributed to some journalists being manhandled by ANC security at the venue. It was disappointing to see. The ANC I knew once led the fight for media freedom but now was employing draconian measures against the media.

I had not encountered Zuma since that fateful Cabinet meeting when my term as CEO of GCIS was summarily ended. Then, at one of the conference sessions, the chairperson announced that Zuma had arrived. Everyone stood up and a section of the hall burst into song. When Zuma walked in, there was a big commotion at the entrance as many of his supporters rushed over to greet him. He spent a bit of time shaking hands and hugging many of the delegates.

As part of the business observer delegation, I happened to be sitting not far from the entrance and the stage. As Zuma made his way to the stage, he reached out to many observers who were shouting for his attention. The next moment I heard a female voice shout, 'Baba, baba!' I looked to see who it was and it turned out to be Duduzile Zuma, the twin sister of Zuma's son Duduzane.

There must have been about five people sitting on my right and Duduzile was about three seats on my left. Zuma walked towards her and started shaking the hands of all the people who were sitting on my right. The only way for him to get to Duduzile would be past me.

I began to feel a little weak, as I had not anticipated any kind of interaction with Zuma at the conference. Would he shake my hand or would he ignore me? He continued walking in my direction and I briefly thought about changing seats with Duduzile. I realised that would be very clumsy and would only draw the attention of the media in attendance. Then, to my great relief, fate intervened and Duduzile rushed forward to meet her father, perhaps thinking his security team would whisk him away before she could give him a hug.

This incident happened on the same day as the announcement of who would be the new ANC president and who would fill the top five positions in the party. Naturally, there was a lot of anticipation. The independent consultant from the company that ran the elections was called to the stage to announce the results. The singing stopped and the room became dead quiet. When Ramaphosa was announced as the new ANC president, half the room exploded in wild singing and the other half fell silent. You could tell that Dlamini-Zuma's supporters were shocked that their candidate had lost.

I couldn't help but look in Zuma's direction to see his reaction, and I noticed that he sat down quietly while the majority of people were on their feet. Zuma remained seated, in a manner that was reminiscent of Mbeki's reaction at the Polokwane conference. Zuma could not hide his disappointment and shock.

The announcement of the remaining top five positions was equally dramatic as it became clear that although the Zuma faction had lost the party presidency, it had managed to win an equal number of the top six positions with the slimmest margin imaginable. Although I respected Dlamini-Zuma as an accomplished ANC leader and public servant, I was and still am convinced that Ramaphosa was the right choice for the ANC and the country. While I celebrated his win as an important step in the fight against corruption and state capture, I also realised that the narrow margin of victory meant that Ramaphosa was going to have a difficult time directing the ANC's fight against those implicated in corruption.

After the conference, the Zuma faction alleged that the election had been stolen, and the Ramaphosa faction claimed that the election of Ace Magashule as party secretary-general had been rigged. The announcement of the secretary-general results was rather embarrassing: the Ramaphosa faction burst into song and lifted former Kwa-Zulu-Natal premier Senzo Mchunu shoulder-high when they thought their candidate had won the vote, only to discover that they had misheard the announcement of the winner. The margin by which Magashule beat Mchunu was a mere 24 votes.

The Free State delegates, whose attendance at the conference had only been confirmed at the last minute after another group lost a court case to declare their attendance unconstitutional, celebrated Magashule's victory as if he had been elected party president. At this point I remembered the words of Fikile Mbalula, who had tweeted in June that year that Magashule's election as ANC secretary-general would be the worst thing that could ever happen to the ANC. Mbalula, who was an NEC member at the time, had tweeted, 'Ace Magashule is a definite no no no, the man will finish what is remaining of our movement. He will kill it.'[50]

On 13 December 2017, three days before the Nasrec conference, ANC national spokesperson Zizi Kodwa had issued a media statement welcoming the Gauteng High Court decision and said that "the judgment brings us a step closer to the implementation of the ANC national executive committee resolution, which directed the judicial commission of inquiry into allegations of state capture be established without delay".[51]

I was one of those who believed that such a resolution would not have seen the light of day had the Zuma faction won the elections outright, because the Zuma faction openly supported his fight against the establishment of the commission of inquiry. The Nasrec conference became a turning point in the country's trajectory, setting the stage for Cyril Ramaphosa to begin his campaign for the presidency of the country and the fight against the capture of the South African state.

On 13 December 2017 the North Gauteng High Court had given Zuma 30 days to appoint the commission of inquiry. In a televised address on 9 January 2018, Zuma announced the establishment of a judicial commission of inquiry into allegations of state capture. I was reminded of the evening at the SABC studio in Hatfield, Pretoria, when former President Mbeki announced his resignation as president following the NEC decision to 'recall' him.

Zuma said, among other things, that 'the allegations that the state has been wrestled out of the hands of its real owners, the people of South Africa, is of paramount importance and are therefore deserving of finality and certainty. It is of such serious public concern that any further delay will make the public doubt government's determination to dismantle all forms of corruption, and entrench the public perception that the state has been captured by private interests for nefarious and self-enrichment purposes.'

He announced that the commission, officially called the Judicial Commission of Inquiry into Allegations of State Capture, would be chaired by Raymond Zondo, Deputy Chief Justice of South Africa. This was a victory for our constitutional democracy and the rule of law. Democratic forces in civil society, the media, opposition parties, business organisations, trade unions and the churches had finally prevailed.

After Ramaphosa's election as ANC president, pressure grew for Zuma to be replaced as the head of state. On 14 February, the day after the police swooped in on the Saxonwold residence of the Gupta family and a day before he was to face a motion of no confidence in Parliament, and after a marathon ANC NEC meeting that had asked him to step down, Zuma resigned as president of the ANC and of the republic. The following day, Ramaphosa was elected by Parliament as the new president of South Africa.

The appointment of the Zondo Commission and Zuma's resignation were two major steps in saving our democracy from the jaws of corrupt forces who were ready to gobble up the state. While I celebrated in silence, I also had to ask myself: how did we get here in the first place?

12

The Zondo Commission

The new year started with the news that MultiChoice, the Naspers-owned company that operates DStv, would not renew its contract with ANN7 and that the channel would therefore no longer be broadcast on the DStv platform once the existing contract expired at the end of August 2018. This followed reports a month earlier that MultiChoice had agreed to increase its annual payment for the ANN7 news channel from R50 million to just over R140 million.[52] MultiChoice was criticised for funding a channel with dwindling viewership that had become known as a 'propaganda machine for the Gupta and Zuma families'.[53] Within months ANN7's fate would be sealed.

Then, in February, the police raided the Guptas' Saxonwold compound, but of course by then the brothers had already left the country. Authorities raided their residence again in April to seize assets as part of the investigations into the Vrede dairy farm case, which arose from allegations that the Guptas had pocketed millions of rands that were intended to support small farmers in the Free State province and had channelled these funds to pay for the notorious Sun City wedding in 2013.

When the regulations of the Zondo Commission were announced in February, it gave the commission the power to, among other things, subpoena witnesses and do searches and seizures. In light of my experience with the ANC's own failed investigation in 2016, I was particularly pleased to see that the commission would have the power to subpoena witnesses and force them to testify under oath.

At his first media briefing as the chairperson of the commission, Justice Raymond Zondo invited anyone with information or evidence of corruption or incidents of state capture to come forward and give evidence. Following the briefing, I was approached by a number of journalists from local and international media institutions who wanted to know if I intended to testify before the commission. I confirmed that I was indeed ready and willing to participate.

Soon thereafter, the commission's legal team made contact with me. They told me I was one of the people they would be inviting to make a formal submission to the commission based on my submission to the Public Protector. My stress level rose as I realised I would be in the public eye again, and there were times when I had to dig deep into my mental resources to find the strength to prepare for the commission processes. Furthermore, it was unpaid work that required many hours of preparation, I also understood that my appearance before the commission would put much pressure on my wife and sons, as well as on my extended family and close friends. However, I was determined to assist the commission in its investigation.

The commission's team advised me that I had to submit an affidavit, which would form part of my testimony, and I decided to seek legal support to ensure that I was well prepared. The only snag was that I couldn't really afford legal representation, but when I reached out to Tyrone Maseko (no relation), an attorney I had seen give commentary to the media on the commission, he gladly agreed to assist me on a pro bono basis. Both Advocate Azhar Bham, an old friend and fellow activist from my student days, and Advocate Dali Mpofu, then chairperson of the EFF, offered their legal services to me on a pro bono basis, but I settled on Maseko and Bham.

At our first meeting with Advocate Paul Pretorius, the commission's evidence leader, and his team we were briefed on the proceedings of the commission and we discussed my affidavit. At the end of the meeting I was a bit shaken when I realised the amount of work I would need to do ahead of my appearance before the commission. I spent many days and weeks trying to source key documents from my previous employers, including GCIS and the Department of Public Service and Administration. I had to do a lot of research, including calling some of the staff I had worked with, reading many newspaper articles and listening to the various interviews I had conducted, in order to gather as much detail as possible. I was required to remember times, dates and venues of all the events I had described in my submissions to the ANC and the Public Protector.

For the first time, I realised what it meant to take the witness stand, even though the commission wasn't a civil or criminal trial. In the end, my legal team's guidance was crucial in helping me prepare for my testimony and they also took me through the process of cross-examination.

The commission's legal team informed me that the hearings would be open to the media. By now I knew that the public interest would bring pressure on me and my family. Phindile paid a heavy price as she watched and supported me through these preparations – being the wife of a whistleblower brought a burden neither she nor I could ever have anticipated.

One day the previous year, I had received a request via my Twitter account to meet with representatives from the police's Directorate for Priority Crime Investigation, or the Hawks as they are commonly known. It turned out that this unit was exploring the possibility of laying formal charges against the Guptas and they wanted me to submit an affidavit. Although I was a bit sceptical of the initiative, I once again decided to cooperate and submit an affidavit, which was basically the same statement I had given to the Public Protector and the ANC.

After the Hawks read my affidavit, they asked me to draw up another one to provide further details that they required, and I duly complied. This was the first time I realised that there was a real possibility of my becoming a state witness in a criminal trial if the Guptas were ever formally charged.

Then, as I was preparing for my appearance before the Zondo Commission in July 2018, I received a call from the Hawks requesting to meet with me again. I assumed it was simply a follow-up meeting and therefore didn't even ask what it was about, although I did check with my attorney whether I should go.

I agreed to meet the Hawks officers at the News Cafe restaurant in Sandton, but when I got there only one of them had arrived. To my surprise, he asked if I had brought my attorney with me. I started to get a bad feeling, and regretted not asking what the meeting would be about. When the second Hawk arrived shortly afterwards, I felt rather intimidated. Here was I, meeting two men who were armed and not in uniform and whose only identification was their business cards. I panicked, as I hadn't told anyone where the meeting would be.

They asked if I wanted to proceed without an attorney being present. I reluctantly agreed to go ahead, despite their warning that everything I said could be used against me in a court of law. Then they told me they were investigating an IT contract I had approved and signed more than 13 years earlier, during my tenure as director-general in the Department of Public Works. They asked me questions about the process that had been followed in the procurement. I told them I couldn't remember much as it had happened such a long time ago, and since I had not been told what the meeting was about I also hadn't prepared.

We concluded the meeting with the understanding that I would make contact with the Department of Public Works to try and get the relevant documentation to help me address their questions, I would retain an attorney and I would prepare a written submission for them. I left the meeting feeling extremely worried because they made it clear to me that I was now the subject of an investigation. I could have kicked myself for being so trusting and agreeing to the meeting without a lawyer being present.

I immediately made contact with Sam Vukela, the director-general in the Department of Public Works, who confirmed that while the matter had been investigated by the Hawks and the Auditor-General at the time, neither investigation had found any irregularities on my part (the project was abandoned after my departure from the department). Vukela was unable to provide Tyrone Maseko with any documentation because all the relevant documents had previously been submitted to the Hawks.

The second meeting with the Hawks took place at their offices in Silverton, Pretoria. This time I was accompanied by Tyrone, and together we viewed the documents but found nothing to suggest any wrongdoing on my part. I didn't hear from the Hawks officers again until the date for my appearance at the Zondo Commission was announced. I then received a call from the Hawks to inform me that the investigation of the 2005 public works IT tender was being reopened.

By then it was common knowledge that the Hawks were one of the state institutions that had been captured during the Zuma era, so I became suspicious about the timing of their 'investigation'. The information about the investigation was also leaked to the media. 'A key witness in Judge Raymond Zondo's inquiry into state capture is being investigated by the Hawks over a contract signed 13 years ago,' one report read.[54]

Following the reports in the media, I received a call from the new head of the Hawks, Lieutenant-General Godfrey Lebeya, to ask for the names of the Hawks officers who had told me I was being investigated, since his office was not aware of the investigation. I gave him the details, and soon thereafter he called back to inform me that his office had no records of either the investigation or the officers who had called me. He told me not to worry any more.

I never again heard from the men who had called me.

I could only conclude that this was a clear case of intimidation.

I had a series of meetings with my lawyers and the commission's legal team ahead of my appearance before the commission. I was fascinated by the fact that, in these meetings, I was often referred to in the third person, and I regularly had to remind them that I was actually present in the room. I definitely learnt a lot about the strange ways of the legal profession. Usually, the meetings ended with my receiving instructions to do more research and to respond to further questions from the commission's legal team.

I tried to watch the live coverage of the commission's first round of hearings, but I found it quite unnerving because of the detailed questions Mcebisi Jonas and Vytjie Mentor had to answer, so I decided to stop watching. As the day of my testimony drew nearer, I found myself sleeping less and less. My legal team helped me to prepare as thoroughly as possible and they advised me to stick to the facts as I recalled them, and to remain calm and focused.

My first appearance was on 30 August 2018.[55] On our way to the building in Parktown where the Zondo Commission sat, Tyrone and Advocate Bham – with whom I had caught a lift – made light conversation but I was so distracted I didn't even hear when they asked me a question. Advocate Bham probably realised I was a bit stressed and he tried to crack a joke or two, but all I wanted was to get it over and done with.

Earlier that morning, I was pleased to receive a call from Tiego Moseneke, the younger brother of former Deputy Chief Justice Dikgang Moseneke, who was a friend and confidant. He wished me good luck and told me I had his unqualified support. 'You should know that you will be representing our generation of activists,' he told me. Although it was a personal call, I knew he represented the views of many activists who had been with me in the trenches during the struggle days.

When we arrived at the commission venue, there was quite a number of journalists ready to take photos. As if I wasn't anxious enough, we learnt on our arrival that my slot had been delayed because Vytjie Mentor had not finished her testimony. So we were ushered into a witness dining area, where we waited for more than two hours. I was starting to get rather agitated – the many cups of coffee and cigarettes didn't help to calm my nerves. I soon realised that the delay meant my testimony wouldn't be completed in one day. In an effort to remain as calm as possible, I deliberately avoided watching the television screen that was broadcasting the hearings.

I was finally called in just before lunch. When I started my testimony, I was so nervous that my throat became very dry and I started coughing. For the first few minutes I struggled to speak without clearing my throat, and the chairperson had to ask me to raise my voice and speak directly into the microphone. The very capable Advocate Vincent Maloka took me through my affidavit, asking many detailed questions and cross-referencing between my submissions to Gwede Mantashe, the Public Protector and the commission. The legal profession has a way of numbering documents that could make your head spin, and it is because of this that I found myself referring to three lever arch files. Maloka would refer me to one file and as soon as I found the relevant paragraph he would already be on another file.

In short, I told the commission about Zuma's call to me shortly before my meeting with Ajay Gupta in Saxonwold, in which he told me to assist the Gupta brothers, and I described what had happened at the meeting with Ajay Gupta.

Towards the end the day, I was really tired and my mouth was incredibly dry. The session adjourned for a short tea break around 3 pm.

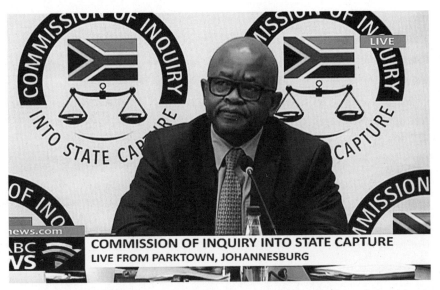

A live SABC broadcast of my appearance at the Zondo Commission.

It was a chance to get some fresh air and drink some coffee, but sadly the commission served what I call 'government-issue coffee', which was tasteless and far too weak for someone in desperate need of a shot of caffeine.

The last round of questions took us to about 4.30 am and by then I couldn't wait for the day to end. I was so tired that at one point it slipped my mind to which president the group of former directors-general that I was a part of had submitted their memorandum about state capture. When Maloka asked the question, my mind just went blank (it was Zuma, of course).

My testimony the following day dealt with the circumstances around my removal from GCIS. I was asked to elaborate on my meeting with Collins Chabane during which he informed me that Zuma had called him with an instruction that I be removed from GCIS by the time he returned to the country from the African Union summit. I also had to describe how my removal from GCIS was communicated to Cabinet and how I ended up being appointed as director-general in the Department of Public Service and Administration. I was at pains to explain that Chabane (who had died in a car accident in 2015) was very unhappy with the decision to remove me, since he was satisfied with my performance as government spokesperson and CEO of GCIS.

Since every implicated person or witness is entitled to have his or her legal representative attend the hearings of the commission, it came as no surprise that I spotted Advocate Muzi Sikhakhane, Zuma's leading legal representative, at the commission on the second day of my testimony. Some people were surprised to see us hugging and cracking jokes. They expected us to be enemies because he was Zuma's advocate. However, Sikhakhane is an old friend of mine, and the fact that we were on different sides of a commission of inquiry didn't mean we had to be enemies. I understood that he was doing his job and we respected each other. It would be foolhardy for me to make enemies of my friends simply because they happened to be representing Zuma.

I was relieved when I finished my testimony, and my legal team and I went out to celebrate what we thought was two successful days before the commission. Judge Zondo's parting words were, 'Mr Maseko, thank you for your testimony but remember that you are still under oath and the commission reserves the right to call you back should the need arise.' It was only then that it dawned on me that I could be called back to the commission at a later stage.

My appearance before the commission was broadcast live and covered extensively in several online and print publications. I continued to receive many requests for interviews, but at least now I had a good excuse to decline them and move out of the limelight. My standard response was that I was still under oath for the rest of the commission's proceedings and not allowed to conduct interviews. Furthermore, my legal team also advised me to not speak to the media.

In July 2019, former President Zuma appeared before the commission for the first time to respond to the many allegations that had been made against him by various witnesses. I deliberately chose not to watch Zuma's testimony because I expected him either to deny everything or to misrepresent the facts.

In responding to questions about my testimony before the commission, Zuma reacted as I thought he would and basically denied everything I had said, including that he had no memory of calling me to ask that I assist the Guptas. When asked whether he had asked Chabane to remove me from GCIS, he denied issuing the instruction and claimed that Chabane was the one who had approached him with a request to transfer me from GCIS because there was conflict between me and Chabane. Incidentally, Zuma also denied meeting Vytjie Mentor at the Gupta Saxonwold residence.

It also appeared as if Zuma wanted to use his appearance before the commission as a platform to 'expose' his detractors by making serious allegations against a number of individuals, including former comrades and certain media personalities. Some of the false and defamatory allegations Zuma made were that Redi Tlhabi, a respected media personality, was a spy who was part of a group of individuals attempting to 'assassinate his character' and that she was making a film about his 2005–2006 rape trial with the aim of furthering the narrative that he was a rapist.[56]

He also claimed that Siphiwe Nyanda, a former chief of the South African National Defence Force and a commander of Umkhonto we Sizwe, and Ngoako Ramatlhodi, a former minister of energy in his Cabinet and a former premier of Limpopo, were apartheid informers. These allegations made headlines, and raised serious questions in my mind about Zuma's integrity, as he had appointed both Nyanda and Ramatlhodi to his Cabinet. Zuma, who had also not submitted an affidavit to the commission, offered no evidence to back up his claims.

In response, Tlhabi approached the Zondo Commission to request the right to cross-examine Zuma. Ramatlhodi and Nyanda rejected the allegations and threatened legal action, with Ramatlhodi saying he would even be prepared to undertake a lie detector test to expose the untruthfulness of the allegations.

Zuma completed his testimony over the course of five days, with the understanding that he would come back to deal with outstanding issues. Zuma successfully avoided further appearances at the commission in October and November of that year, in one instance citing health reasons and in the other that he needed more time to prepare for both the commission and his corruption trial, which was due to take place at the same time in the Pietermaritzburg High Court.

Following Zuma's testimony, I received a letter from the commission requesting that I submit an affidavit responding to his response to my testimony, which I duly complied with. In my affidavit, I said that Chabane and I had had a solid working relationship and that Zuma was not telling the truth when he suggested that Chabane was the one who had approached him requesting that I be transferred from GCIS. Evidence was produced showing that Chabane was not only satisfied with my performance but had in fact given me an above-average performance score. I also mentioned that Chabane and I had had a social relationship, which included us regularly playing golf together.

In early December 2019, it was former Minister of Public Service and Administration Richard Baloyi's turn to testify before the commission. Baloyi testified that Chabane had approached him to request my transfer from GCIS to the Department of Public Service and Administration and that he had not only agreed but had also facilitated my transfer.

Baloyi also disputed that he and I had had a disagreement that led to my departure. He implied that I had suggested that his conduct and attitude towards me, as his accounting officer, meant that he was somehow involved in state capture.

Once again, the commission's lawyers reached out to me via my legal team and requested that I submit yet another affidavit, this time in response to Baloyi's testimony. As before, I had to drop everything to prepare a responding affidavit. In dealing with his assertion that he had facilitated my move from GCIS to public service and administration, I pointed out that I was the person who had called Baloyi after that fateful Cabinet meeting to inform him that I was his new director-general, and that he was not only unaware of the move but was also shocked and upset that he had not been consulted before the decision was made. I mentioned that he only facilitated the move *after* the decision to move me from GCIS had already been made.

When I subsequently appeared before the commission to clarify certain issues raised in Baloyi's affidavit, I was shocked to see that the letter submitted by Baloyi's legal team, which purported to be a request by Chabane for my transfer, had been tampered with, and the date altered. I pointed this out to the chairperson of the commission.

I concurred with Baloyi that we didn't have a disagreement. However, in my responding affidavit I pointed out that he never made me feel welcome in his department, and that I had been excluded from important meetings and discussions that I was supposed to have been part of as an accounting officer.

Initially, when I decided to testify before the commission I expected to appear before Judge Zondo only once, but I ended up appearing three times. At the end of each round of testimony, the judge would thank me for attending and assisting the commission with its work, and remind me that I might be called upon to testify again in the future.

Over the months that followed my first appearance, I started to worry about the time I was spending writing affidavits and, more importantly, about the amount of time that my legal team was spending on the matter without getting paid for it. I was therefore pleased to hear that none of the parties I had mentioned in my testimony had applied to cross-examine me.

At the time of writing this book, there was still no clear indication as to whether the Guptas would ever be extradited to South Africa to account for their role in state capture. While there have been denials made through the media, the Gupta family has refused to formally answer the allegations that have been made against them in the Public Protector's 'State of Capture' report and in the numerous affidavits that have been submitted to the Zondo Commission. It is of great concern that we may not be able to recover at least part of the taxpayers' money that was illicitly taken out of our country.

There are concerns by some that the Zondo Commission's findings might not lead to prosecutions, but I believe the commission has played a crucial role in giving the South African public an understanding of the phenomenon of state capture. It is important to understand how this form of corruption unfolded and who the key decision-makers, facilitators and beneficiaries were, how the flow of funds worked and what the impact on government's service delivery was. The Zondo Commission has shown us how the political elite was bought by a single family and how their power over the head of state led to a number of state institutions and entities being looted and almost destroyed.

In a positive development, President Cyril Ramaphosa amended the commission's regulations in mid-2020 to give the NPA access to the commission's investigations. This cleared the way for the commission's staff and investigators to share information and resources with their fellow corruption-busters in government, such as the NPA's Investigating Directorate, which is tasked with building cases against those implicated in state capture.[57] This will help law enforcement agencies to arrest and prosecute implicated parties and hopefully recover some of the stolen public resources. Even if not all the instances of corruption are prosecuted, the findings of the Zondo Commission will hopefully encourage government and civil society to push for legislative changes that will bring about greater accountability.

Ultimately, though, South Africans want to see people being held to account for state capture, and the litmus test will be the number of individuals who are arrested and successfully prosecuted. In part, this will depend on how effectively the NPA and the South African Police Service act on the findings and recommendations of the Zondo Commission. My hope is that in having a better understanding of how state capture happened, we will be in a better position to avoid it in future.

Following my testimony before the commission, I received widespread support from family, friends and my former government colleagues, most of whom congratulated me for my courage. My response was that it was the right thing to do, and I expressed the hope that more of my ex-colleagues would also be willing to make submissions to the commission. In fact, during my testimony, Justice Zondo asked if I was aware of any other government officials who had had similar experiences regarding state capture. I replied that there were indeed officials who were willing to speak up, and I tabled the statement signed by 27 former directors-general who I expected to come forward. I was pleased to see a number of my ex-colleagues from GCIS being brave enough to make submissions to the Zondo Commission. I was most encouraged and humbled by members of the public who were always willing to pass on a compliment and give me a pat on the back for speaking out. When asked why I had done it, my response was, 'I did it for my country.'

I noticed a bit of a sea change in attitudes towards me from a number of quarters, including civil society organisations such as the Nelson Mandela Foundation and the Ahmed Kathrada Foundation. I even got an invitation to join the Council for the Advancement of the South African Constitution. However, the biggest acknowledgement came from the Ahmed Kathrada Foundation, which organised an event to recognise all those who had come forward to expose state capture. I, together with other brave South Africans, including Mcebisi Jonas,

Vytjie Mentor and others, were given awards at a dinner in Sandton. This was my first public gathering in a long time, as I had deliberately avoided such events.

The majority of ANC comrades continued to give me their distant support, especially through the now-popular WhatsApp groups, even though there were some in these groups who were unhappy about ANC comrades speaking out about government corruption. Although I generally welcome debate, I found it a bit exhausting that some of the participants in these groups came across as defending state capture out of loyalty to this or that faction. I opted to mute many of these groups, and instead opted for Twitter because I found it to have 'expected toxicity' as opposed to the political grandstanding that I found on WhatsApp.

There were a number of ANC leaders, who had clearly aligned themselves to the Zuma faction, such as Tony Yengeni and Mzwandile Masina, the mayor of Ekurhuleni, who used social media platforms such as Twitter to openly criticise those of us who had decided to make submissions to the Zondo Commission by calling us liars. I observed and tolerated their abuse until I watched a debate on Newzroom Afrika in which Masina blatantly accused me of lying about Zuma. I lost my cool and decided to call in to the show and challenge Masina on his lies and for misleading the public. My argument with him spilled over onto Twitter and he ended up threatening me physically in public. I was more than flabbergasted that a public official could make threats on a social media platform. I suppose I could have reported him to the ANC's Integrity Committee, which I did not do because such actions are reserved for active ANC members. I simply invited him to carry through with his threat, which he never did.

Naturally, there were a number of critiques, including from many Twitter Einsteins who never missed an opportunity to call me all kinds of names and hurl profanities in my direction. I ignored most of it. I was called *impimpi* (informer), **umdlwembe** (undisciplined person or traitor) and askari, and some even went to the extent of threatening me with violence. But I had developed a thick skin by then and remained resolute and calm. In fact, these insults reminded me of when I was head of the Gauteng Department of Education: during a protest march to my offices, members of the South African Democratic Teachers' Union carried placards bearing shocking and unprintable slogans about me. I had just ignored them too.

I was also inundated with requests for interviews from numerous media houses, and I agreed to do a few until my legal team of Bham and Maseko reminded me that I was still under oath and could be called back to the stand, and that it was not advisable for me to conduct interviews. I accepted their advice with pleasure because it helped to take away the pressure and to give me a chance to stand back and get a bit of rest.

The Guptas had already skipped the country by then, and they declined any request to appear before the commission because they feared they would be arrested. Naturally, they denied all the allegations against them and claimed it was all lies. I had looked forward to facing Ajay Gupta and telling him to his face that he had tried to strongarm me into breaking the law by illegally forcing GCIS and other government departments to hand over their advertising budget to him and his brothers. I was encouraged by media reports indicating that the Department of Justice was in the process of approaching the authorities in Dubai to extradite the Guptas. But the jury is still out on whether the Guptas or the G-Force will ever return to South Africa to face justice.

Postscript

WHEN I JOINED the struggle as a child in Soweto, I never imagined that one day I would end up blowing the whistle on a special kind of corruption that was destroying my beloved ANC and the values I have been fighting for all my life.

I consider myself a child of the ANC. Of all the liberation movements, I was most attracted to the ANC because it had adopted the Freedom Charter as its guiding document, and I believed it had the right ideological and strategic vision for liberating the country. As an activist for great parts of my youth and young adulthood, my only goal in life was to be of service to my country. The ANC offered the vehicle through which I could fulfil this goal.

My work on the ground and my meetings with ANC leaders both inside and outside the country reaffirmed my decision to be part of what I considered to be a glorious movement. My struggle activities brought me into contact with committed, selfless fellow activists and leaders of the Mass Democratic Movement and eventually leaders of the ANC.

Joining the struggle during apartheid was very risky, and many activists lost their lives in the process. Families lost breadwinners. Many people went into exile and some spent many days, months and years in apartheid prisons so that our country could be free. These struggle experiences produced the most dedicated, principled, honest and patriotic South Africans, who were committed to building a truly non-racial, non-sexist and democratic South Africa.

My time as a political activist shaped my political, philosophical and ideological outlook on life – my very being as a person. My activism was built on strong principles, a specific view of the world and, most importantly, an ethical outlook. It strengthened my love for my country, for South Africans of all races and cultural backgrounds, and my commitment to making a difference. This is also what made me decide to study law: I believed that, as a lawyer, I could use the legal system to help the disempowered, poor and disadvantaged.

Under Madiba a spirit of service reigned, and the political initiative of Batho Pele (People First) was adopted. But soon things started to change. Leaders, especially ministers, started behaving like god-like figures, driven around by chauffeurs, with security guards on hand to carry their bags, open doors and even drive their kids to school. One of the first controversies of the democratic era was the high level of expenditure on cars for ministers and their deputies, and soon the term 'gravy train' became part of public parlance.

The allegations of corruption in the 1999 arms deal were deeply upsetting to me, as these allegedly involved the highest levels of both government and the ANC. Senior government figures, such as Tony Yengeni, then chairperson of the parliamentary portfolio committee on defence, and Jacob Zuma, then MEC for economic affairs in KwaZulu-Natal, were accused of corruption. In recent years, I was shocked by the scandal pertaining to the more than R250 million spent on renovating Zuma's private residence at Nkandla.

What disappointed me most was the way the ANC responded to these allegations, and later also to those around state capture. In the case of Nkandla, ANC MPs came out in full support of Zuma as their president, and Cabinet ministers went to absurd lengths to shield him from public scrutiny. One of the most embarrassing developments was in May 2015 when Cabinet ministers held a media conference at which they tried to claim, among other things, that a swimming pool built at Nkandla with taxpayers' money was supposedly a 'fire pool' that could be used to extinguish a fire at the residence.[58]

In my view, this was one of the low points in the ANC government's history. It is unbelievable to think that ministers could stoop so low to defend a leader who was obviously in the wrong.

It seems that the party is incapable of holding its leaders to account. In 2016 Bathabile Dlamini, then president of the ANC Women's League and a staunch Zuma supporter, even discouraged ANC members from airing the party's dirty laundry in public with the warning that 'all of us in the NEC has smallanyana skeletons and we don't want to take out skeletons because all hell will break loose'.[59]

The ANC appears to be in a quandary because many of those facing serious corruption allegations of late are senior office bearers, such as Ace Magashule, secretary-general of the party. There are only two occasions that I am aware of where the ANC has taken action against one of its top six leaders: the first was when Thabo Mbeki fired Zuma as his deputy president and the second was when Mbeki was recalled as president by the NEC.

Sadly, reports of alleged corruption continue to this day, affecting all spheres of government. We have reached the stage where the true costs of corruption are starting to be felt and experienced by all South Africans in all corners of our country. These range from potholes the size of splash pools, shortages of classrooms, a lack of toilet facilities at schools, endless load shedding, water shortages and municipalities that are unable to pay salaries due to mismanagement of funds. This is due to a dwindling economy and an empty public purse. Once again, the poorest of the poor have to bear the brunt.

Corruption has long-term and far-reaching consequences, and the biggest losers are always the poorest of the poor. Every rand that leaves government coffers illegally could be used to build a toilet at a rural school, set up a new clinic, fix a burst water pipe or a pothole, help to pay off the country's debt or supply personal protective equipment to hospitals. Corruption comes down to stealing from the poor who have voted the ANC into office.

The ANC I joined and knew as a young activist would not have allowed all of this to happen. The ANC of Albert Luthuli, Oliver Tambo, Walter Sisulu, Nelson Mandela, Joe Slovo, Ahmed Kathrada, Albertina Sisulu and Winnie Madikizela-Mandela must be looking down on us with utter disappointment for destroying what they bequeathed to us.

For some time after I left the public service in 2011, I thought I would go to my grave with the story of how the G-Force tried to bully me into breaking government procurement rules and regulations and President Jacob Zuma's suggestion that I help his Gupta friends. One of the reasons it took me a while to speak out was because it wasn't easy for me to expose one of the leaders I had hero-worshipped for the greater part of my life. Zuma was one of the leaders of the party that had liberated my beloved country, and as head of state he was one of the most powerful people on the continent.

For a long time, I thought that my experience with the Guptas and Zuma was an isolated case. That was until I realised that the country was being stolen and torn apart by two families that were prepared to break every rule in the book to amass as much wealth as possible, all the while claiming they were advancing radical economic transformation in the interests of the poor. They also didn't care that they were putting the country's economic future at risk. This corruption was not limited to the government sphere. As the testimony before the Zondo Commission has shown, many private companies not only benefited from but actively aided state capture.

At the end of the Mbeki era, the primary debate about the two centres of power focused on Luthuli House, the ANC headquarters, as the political centre and the Union Buildings as the *de jure* centre of state power. Under Zuma's tenure, two additional centres emerged: Nkandla and Saxonwold.

Nkandla became known as the go-to place when Zuma's off-the-radar support was needed for something. Many businesspeople visited and wanted to be seen at Nkandla to seek or receive Zuma's blessing for business opportunities that required either government support or regulatory changes. The most popular time to visit was in December, when Zuma held an annual event for the Jacob Zuma Foundation. Hordes of politicians and businesspeople would attend in the hope of securing an audience with Zuma.

After my encounters with the Guptas in 2010 I was advised to visit Nkandla to 'apologise' and to rebuild my relationship with Zuma, but I politely declined. Years later, I suggested on Twitter that if everyone who had ever been to the Gupta residence were to gather, the FNB Stadium would not be big enough to accommodate them. However, if all those who had descended on Nkandla over the years to meet Zuma were to gather, they would fill the stadium twice.

The Guptas' Saxonwold residence became the fourth centre of power. Reports and affidavits submitted to the Zondo Commission suggest that key government appointments, including of ministers and the heads of SOEs, as well as government contracts, were discussed and decided upon by, or with the input of, the Guptas. In my specific case, I was summoned to Saxonwold to discuss government budgets, with express endorsement from Zuma that I should help the Gupta brothers. The Saxonwold residence was clearly a centre of power that eclipsed both the Union Buildings and Luthuli House. This gave rise to an alternative state alongside the actual state.

I was encouraged to share my experiences when a number of South Africans started speaking out about incidents that pointed to state capture by the Guptas. I realised that I was not alone. Individuals such as Mcebisi Jonas and Vytjie Mentor have spoken out at great risk to themselves and their families. The indications are that the looters of our state coffers would not hesitate to intimidate, or even kill, if their interests are threatened. That is why these whistleblowers, and the others who have spoken out, are true heroes and heroines in my opinion.

I spent at least three years sharing my experience only with friends and family, especially my wife. When I finally decided to go public with my story, it was because I saw it as my responsibility to expose the lies that were being told by Zuma and his Gupta friends. I still thought of myself as a public servant who owed his loyalty to the Constitution and to the citizens of South Africa whose freedom I had fought for.

So why did I blow the whistle on Zuma and the Guptas? Because I refused to be part of a scheme that was blatantly aimed at stealing from the poor. I was not prepared to be part of a government that was run by individuals who abused their positions and connections to the head of state to enrich themselves and their families. Too many South Africans lost their lives in the fight against apartheid and colonialism, and I was not prepared to sell this hard-won freedom for a few pennies. To have cooperated with the Guptas would have meant betraying the revolution.

However, I must confess that I did not fully realise the impact that speaking out about state capture would have on me and my family. It came at a great cost, as I soon became a professional, political and social leper, shunned by friends and enemies alike. After leaving the public service, I thought the best way forward financially was to set myself up as an entrepreneur, but I had become a politically exposed person,[60] a marked man. This meant that fundraising for any business venture or investment attracted extra scrutiny from financial institutions, scrutiny that extended to cases where I wanted to make investments. In the words of one of the institutions I applied to: 'Due to the client being a prominent and influential person we are obliged to perform enhanced due diligence. I want to emphasise that this is a regulatory obligation placed on us and we are sensitive to the inconvenience and intrusion on Mr Maseko.'

Soon the haunting calls of creditors started ringing and the banks started calling in loans and overdrafts. It was the echo of a whistle blown. It is painfully true that a principle is not a principle until it costs you money. My creditors didn't care about my crusade to expose corruption. To them, I was simply one of the thousands of bad debtors who had to be pursued relentlessly. At the beginning of 2017, things were getting really tough as my debts were piling up. It dawned on me that my last formal salary had been in 2011 when I left the public service. Pawn shops became my unimaginable friends. Days became longer and nights became my enemy as sleep evaded me. At one point alcohol and cigarettes found their way onto my list of bad habits. Occasional visits to church did not help either.

Despite my 17 years of experience in the public service and my many qualifications, which included senior executive certificates from Wits University and Harvard, the private sector was hesitant to employ me, and it seemed unlikely that I would ever get an appointment in the public service again. My profile as a whistleblower meant that I could not even get board appointments.

I reached out to a number of friends and former comrades who I thought might be willing to help. Some never responded to my calls, and the few who did asked me to send them my CV, but nothing ever came of it. Only the late Jackson Mthembu, once minister in the Presidency, Trevor Manuel, former minister of finance, and Pravin Gordhan, the minister of public enterprises, were bravely willing to assist in concrete ways. Gordhan, for instance, was able to accommodate me for a few months in his office, while Manuel opened channels with Old Mutual employees who were willing to talk to me.

*At a post-Cabinet media briefing in 2010 with Minister Pravin Gordhan (left),
one of the few politicians who assisted me after I left the government.*

Being in this position struck the pillars of my resolve and shook me
to the core. There were days when courage and hope seemed to fail me.
The journey a whistleblower goes on is mostly a lonely one. My refuges
became reading, playing golf, going to the gym and becoming a Twitter
activist. I accepted that life would never be the same for me again.

Fortunately, one of the investments I made yielded after a while,
and I was able to breathe a little easier. Also, by the time I decided to
speak out, my children had nearly finished with school. I pulled
through mainly because of the help of a number of loyal friends and
the unwavering support of Phindile, my sons, a few friends and my
extended family. The many members of the public who would stop me
on the street or in shopping malls to offer their support, despite the
attacks I endured on social media, also helped to carry me through.

While I refused to be intimidated by faceless dark forces, I couldn't
help but be affected by the many threats I received from anonymous
callers. At the time I did not have the mental energy to report these
calls to the police, but, looking back, I realise that I should have. Many

people have asked me if I was at any point scared for my life for defying the Gupta brothers. While there were times when I feared for my safety and that of my family, I told myself that I would rather die for the truth than live for lies.

During these times I couldn't help but think of Noby Ngombane, a friend and comrade I served with in the national executive committee of Azaso. Noby was a senior official in the Free State premier's office when he was shot in cold blood in 2005 outside his home in Bloemfontein, apparently for exposing corruption in the province.

However, despite all the challenges I have faced over the past few years, at no stage did I regret my refusal both to cooperate with the Guptas and to obey Zuma's request to help them. The only regret I have is that I didn't go to a police station immediately after my meeting with Ajay Gupta at the Saxonwold house and report his unlawful demand.

I remain a proud public servant, and I find courage in the fact that I have never given up the principles of the struggle nor my belief that my actions have helped to serve the greater good. I want to encourage honest civil servants and citizens in the private sector to speak out when they become aware of unlawful actions. Our young democracy must be rid of the culture of corruption that is ripping the country and our social fabric apart. My hope is that this book will encourage rather than discourage them. As Mandy Wiener's book *The Whistleblowers* has shown, the corrupt will never be held accountable for their deeds without these individuals.[61]

The media, particularly investigative journalists such as those at Scorpio and amaBhungane, should also be recognised for their role in exposing corruption in general and state capture in particular. The role of Chapter 9 institutions such as the Public Protector and the Auditor-General, the courts, and civil society organisations such as the Nelson Mandela Foundation, Ahmed Kathrada Foundation, Corruption Watch, Section 21 and opposition parties needs to be recognised and acknowledged. These bodies have played a significant role in the fight against state capture, exposing corruption in general and demanding accountability from those in positions of authority. Sadly, Parliament was generally found wanting when it came to holding the executive and public servants to account.

I could have kept quiet, left the public service and secured myself a cushy job in the private sector and gone to the grave with my story, but my conscience would have haunted me. For the sake of those who made the ultimate sacrifice in the struggle against oppression, I could not keep quiet. I was part of a generation of activists who were prepared to sacrifice their lives for the freedom of the oppressed.

I spent all my adult life working in the public service to transform our society so that our young democracy could be a shining example of how to address poverty, inequality and subjugation. If you had asked me as a young activist, I would never have imagined that one day I would be considered an enemy of the state for exposing graft. But if anyone asks me whether I would do it again, my answer would be an emphatic *yes*.

In my own way, I will continue to be of service to this nation, and I will campaign for legislation to enable citizens to expose wrongdoing without suffering such personal consequences. I will use my remaining days to help create an institution to support whistleblowers and their families. This support will include providing security, legal advice, income protection and education support.

Speaking out against wrongdoing and corruption is the duty of every citizen who cares about the future of our democracy. In everything we do, we should strive to be good, patriotic citizens.

My journey so far hasn't always been easy, but it has been worth it. I leave it to history to judge me.

Nkosi sikelel' iAfrika – may God bless Africa.

Annexure

Statement by 27 former directors-general

A Voice of Reason
'Save the Soul of the Public Service from State Capture'

22 April 2016

Addressed to:

Minister of Finance, Minister Pravin Gordhan, MP
Minister of Public Service and Administration, Minister Ngaoko Ramatlhodi, MP
Cc: The President of the Republic of South Africa
       The Deputy President of the Republic of South Africa

We, the undersigned, are former Directors General in the post-apartheid South African government, with a prior history in the liberation struggle where we served as cadres of Umkhonto we Sizwe, officials of the African National Congress (ANC), Azanian People's Organisation (AZAPO), the Pan Africanist Congress (PAC), and various organisations of the Mass Democratic Movement.

We were privileged, honoured and challenged to serve in various capacities at the inception of the new democratic government, in particular as Directors General from 1994. We served in our individual capacities as public servants, for periods ranging between 3 years to 15 years each in single or multiple departments. We played a role in the early efforts to transform the South African State into a more effective organ to achieve the aspirations and transformatory goals of the liberation struggle and the new democratic government to ensure a better life for our people and to address the inequities and injustices of the past.

In pursuit of the above, we believe we upheld the principles of the Constitution, and were guided primarily by the founding legislation for public sector management – the Public Service Act of 1994 [PSA] as amended and the Public Finance Management Act (Act 1 of 1999) [PFMA].

We submit this memorandum to express our collective concern at recent revelations of state capture by the Gupta family, their apparent influence over political and administrative appointments, and their involvement in the irregular facilitation, securing and issuing of government tenders and contracts. We also express our concern at the effect of the recent Constitutional Court judgement in the Nkandla matter on the legitimacy of the State and its ability to focus resources and efforts on delivering services to our people, growing the economy and achieving our transformatory and developmental goals.

Whilst noting the initiative undertaken by the ANC to conduct an internal inquiry we as former accounting officers believe that, to the extent that the issues raised are of an administrative nature, there are adequate provisions within the PFMA and PSA that make it obligatory for these allegations to be addressed.

We therefore call for the establishment of an Independent Public Inquiry in terms of Section 4(1)(a) of the Promotion of Administrative Justice Act to include representatives of Chapter 9 institution such as the Public Protector and Auditor General and the Chapter 10 institution – the Public Service Commission, as well as accountants, retired judges, advocates and experts on international financial flows.

This inquiry should investigate all senior political and administrative officials who may, in their dealings with the Guptas and associated companies, have contravened the Constitution, the PFMA and the Public Service Act as amended. We strongly recommend that this Commission be established within three months and give a public progress report within six months.

We believe that there is adequate provision in existing statutes to mitigate corruptive practices and ensure good governance. However, in our view the reported allegations of Gupta involvement in Ministerial appointments, manipulation of awarding of tenders, appointment of Gupta-nominated individuals to strategic positions, show possible legislative breach. These include but are not limited to:

- Section 91(2) of the Constitution;
- Section 96 (1) and (2a, b, and c) and Schedule 2 of the Constitution;
- Chapter 10 of the Constitution, Section 195(1);
- Chapter 10, section 195(4) of the Constitution;
- Section 64 of the PFMA Act.

We note and welcome the initiatives of the Minister of Finance and the National Treasury to investigate existing contracts involving the Guptas. We call upon the Auditor General and Chief Procurement Officer to further investigate all government tenders and contracts awarded to Gupta-associated companies to assess their compliance with the PFMA Act and Regulations and the Preferential Procurement Policy Framework Act of 2000 and Regulations.

We call upon the Public Service Commission to investigate all irregular or suspicious appointments of public servants in critical positions of Directors General, Ministerial Chiefs of Staff, Heads of Procurement Units, Members of Bid Specification Committees, Bid Evaluation Committees and Bid Adjudication Committees.

We also call upon the National Treasury to initiate an investigation into the possible involvement of the Guptas and associated companies in illicit financial flows out of South Africa and recommend the appointment of an independent research institution to assist in this investigation.

We call upon the Minister of the Public Service and Administration to create an enabling environment to allow all public servants to act in terms of the existing prescripts and to freely come forward to provide information to the Public Inquiry as well as to report any breaches of the relevant legislation, regulations and codes of conduct.

Signed by:

Frank Chikane

Barry Gilder

Ketso Gordhan

Thozi Gwanya

Roger Jardine

Themba Maseko

Mzuvukile Maqetuka

Mogopodi Mokoena

Itumeleng Mosala

Mpumi Mpofu

Mavuso Msimang

Andile Ngcaba

Gibson Njenje

Bongiwe Njobe

Ayanda Ntsaluba

Siphiwe Nyanda

Dipak Patel

Mallele Petje

Vusi Pikoli

Sipho Pityana

Alistair Ruiters

Sipho Shabalala

Xoliswa Sibeko

Moe Shaik

Lyndall Shope-Mafole

Vincent Zwelibanzi Mntambo

Pam Yako

Endnotes

CHAPTER 1

1   Brand South Africa, 'New board for Brand South Africa', 21 January 2010, www.brandsouthafrica.com/south-africa-fast-facts/media-facts/new-board-for-brand-south-africa.

2   Adriaan Basson and Pieter du Toit, *Enemy of the People: How Jacob Zuma Stole South Africa and How the People Fought Back* (Johannesburg: Jonathan Ball Publishers, 2017).

CHAPTER 3

3   Truth and Reconciliation Commission, Final Report, vol 2, chapter 2, subsection 36, sabctrc.saha.org.za/reports/volume2/chapter2/subsection36.htm?t=%2Bshabangu+%2Bportia&tab=report.

4   Ibid.

5   Ibid.

CHAPTER 4

6   Scott Kraft, 'Bomb kills ANC lawyer who tracked hit squads', *Los Angeles Times*, 17 February 1991, www.latimes.com/archives/la-xpm-1991-02-17-mn-2173-story.html; Terry Bell and Dumisa Buhle Ntsebeza, *Unfinished Business: South Africa, Apartheid and Truth* (London: Verso, 2003); and entry for Bheki Mlangeni on South African History Online, 4 October 2019, www.sahistory.org.za/people/bheki-mlangeni#:~:text=Location%20of%20Death%3A&text=On%2017%20November%201989%2C%20prompted,South%20African%20Police's%20death%20squad.

7   Testimony of Catherine Mlangeni and Sepati Mlangeni before the Truth and Reconciliation Commission, 2 May 1996, www.justice.gov.za/trc/hrvtrans/methodis/mlangeni.htm.

CHAPTER 5

8   See Janet Kathyola, 'The political-administrative interface: The key to good public sector governance and effectiveness in Commonwealth Africa', in *Commonwealth Good Governance 2010/2011: Developing Capacity in the Public Sector* (London: Commonwealth Secretariat, 2010).

CHAPTER 6

9   Human Rights Watch, 'South Africa: Events of 2008', Human Rights Watch World Report 2009, www.hrw.org/world-report/2009/country-chapters/south-africa.
10 GCIS, 'Government on suspension of the National Director of Public Prosecutions, Vusi Pikoli', official government statement, 24 September 2007, www.gov.za/government-suspension-national-director-public-prosecutions-v-pikoli.
11 Karyn Maughan and Gill Gifford, 'Pikoli fired for Mbeki snub', Independent Online, 9 December 2008, www.iol.co.za/news/pikoli-fired-for-mbeki-snub-428340.

CHAPTER 7

12 Jan-Jan Joubert, 'The fall of Thabo Mbeki', Politicsweb, 5 February 2008, www.politicsweb.co.za/news-and-analysis/the-fall-of-thabo-mbeki.
13 Ibid.
14 Frank Chikane, *Eight Days in September: The Removal of Thabo Mbeki* (Johannesburg: Picador Africa, 2012).
15 Entry for Dr Mantombazana 'Manto' Tshabalala-Msimang, South African History Online, 16 November 2020, www.sahistory.org.za/people/dr-mantombazana-manto-tshabalala-msimang.
16 Gareth van Onselen, 'Political Musical Chairs: Turnover in the Executive and Administration since 2009', report by the Institute of Race Relations, August 2017, irr.org.za/reports/occasional-reports/files/irr-political-musical-chairs.pdf.

CHAPTER 8

17 Pieter-Louis Myburgh, *The Republic of Gupta: A Story of State Capture* (Johannesburg: Penguin, 2017).

CHAPTER 9

18 'Themba Maseko bows out', SA News.gov.za, 3 February 2011, www.sanews.gov.za/south-africa/themba-maseko-bows-out.

CHAPTER 10

19 Barry Bateman and Gia Nicolaides, 'Gupta family gets royal escort', EWN, 30 April 2013, ewn.co.za/2013/04/30/Gupta-family-gets-royal-SA-escort.
20 'ANC statement on the landing at Waterfkloof', issued by Gwede Mantashe, 30 April 2013, www.politicsweb.co.za/party/sandf-must-explain-why-gupta-plane-allowed-to-land.

21 Jeanette Chabalala, 'Waterkloof landing: "I abused the powers of my office," Koloane admits', News24, 9 July 2019, www.news24.com/news24/SouthAfrica/News/waterkloof-landing-i-abused-the-powers-of-my-office-koloane-admits-20190709.

22 Rebecca Davis, 'I lied about Zuma involvement in Waterkloof, Bruce Koloane claims', *Daily Maverick*, 9 July 2019, www.dailymaverick.co.za/article/2019-07-09-newsflash-i-lied-about-zuma-involvement-in-waterkloof-bruce-koloane-claims/.

23 Chikane, *Eight Days in September*, p 307.

24 Staff reporter, 'ANC: Nothing wrong with Zuma's call for support from business', *Mail & Guardian*, 15 January 2013, mg.co.za/article/2013-01-15-00-anc-backs-zuma-for-business-support-comment/.

25 Mcebisi Jonas, 'Media statement by deputy minister of finance, Mr Mcebisi Jonas,' issued on behalf of the Ministry of Finance, 16 March 2016, www.news24.com/news24/SouthAfrica/News/full-text-mcebisi-jonas-statement-20160316-2.

26 Mcebisi Jonas, 'Statement to the Inquiry into State Capture', 8 August 2018, www.corruptionwatch.org.za/wp-content/uploads/2018/08/386958764-State-Capture-Inquiry-Mcebisi-Jonas-s-full-statement.pdf; Andrew England, 'S Africa minister alleges Guptas offered him Treasury chief role', *Financial Times*, 16 March 2016, www.ft.com/content/76f6b6dc-eb90-11e5-888e-2eadd5fbc4a4.

27 Thanduxolo Jika, Qaanitah Hunter and Sabelo Skiti, 'How Guptas shopped for new minister', *Sunday Times*, 13 March 2016, www.timeslive.co.za/sunday-times/news/2016-03-13-how-guptas-shopped-for-new-minister/.

28 Ibid.

29 Stuart Lowman, 'State capture? Former ANC MP claims Guptas offered PE minister role', *BizNews*, 15 March 2016, www.biznews.com/leadership/2016/03/15/former-anc-mp-gutpas-offered-minister-role-exchange-saa-route-india.

30 EWN reporter, 'Julius "got your files" Malema', EWN, 16 February 2016, ewn.co.za/2016/02/16/Julius-got-your-files-Malema.

31 Qaanitah Hunter and Sibongakonke Shoba, '"Zuma told me to help Guptas"', *Sunday Times*, 20 March 2016, www.timeslive.co.za/sunday-times/news/2016-03-20-zuma-told-me-to-help-guptas/.

32 Govan Whittles, 'Members who speak out against the Guptas will be protected politically', EWN, 21 March 2016, ewn.co.za/2016/03/21/ANC-to-protect-those-that-spoke-up-about-Zuma-Gupta-influence.

33 Mpho Raborife, 'ANC got only 1 written complaint on state capture – Mantashe', News24, 31 May 2016, www.news24.com/news24/SouthAfrica/Politics/anc-only-got-1-written-complaint-on-state-capture-mantashe-20160531.

34 Ibid.

35 Stuart Lowman, 'Full statement: 27 former DGs call for "state capture" enquiry. Silence betrays trust', Fin24, 16 May 2016, www.news24.com/fin24/biznews/full-statement-27-former-dgs-call-for-state-capture-inquiry-silence-betrays-trust-20160516.

36 Ibid.

CHAPTER 11

37 Genevieve Quintal, 'Gupta-owned media agree to publish broadcast apology: ANC', TimesLive, 23 March 2016, www.timeslive.co.za/politics/2016-03-23-gupta-owned-media-agree-to-publish-broadcast-apology-anc/.

38 Fin24 reporter, 'Department spent close to R1m on single Gupta-sponsored breakfast', News24, 6 June 2017, www.news24.com/fin24/tech/companies/department-spent-close-to-r1m-on-single-gupta-sponsored-breakfast-20170606.

39 Agency staff, 'Five ANN7 journalists fired', TechCentral, 4 August 2016, tech-central.co.za/5-ann7-journalists-fired/67479/.

40 Public Protector South Africa, 'State of Capture', report no: 6 of 2016/17, 14 October 2016, www.saflii.org/images/329756472-State-of-Capture.pdf.

41 Thandeka Gqubule, *No Longer Whispering to Power: The Story of Thuli Madonsela* (Johannesburg: Jonathan Ball Publishers, 2017).

42 Pierre de Vos, 'Analysis: Review of State Capture report – the legal issues', *Daily Maverick*, 26 November 2016, www.dailymaverick.co.za/article/2016-11-26-analysis-review-of-state-capture-report-the-legal-issues/.

43 Dineo Bendile, 'ANC calls for judicial commission of inquiry into state capture', *Mail & Guardian*, 27 May 2017, mg.co.za/article/2017-05-29-anc-calls-for-judicial-commission-of-inquiry-into-state-capture/.

44 Ibid.

45 Ibid.

46 See *Economic Freedom Fighters v Speaker of the National Assembly and Others; Democratic Alliance v Speaker of the National Assembly and Others* [2016] ZACC 11, Constitutional Court of South Africa, cases 143/15 and 171/15, cdn.24.co.za/files/Cms/General/d/3834/24efe59744c642a1a02360235f4d026b.pdf.

47 *President of the Republic of South Africa v Office of the Public Protector and Others*, Pretoria High Court, 13 December 2017, www.saflii.org/za/cases/ZAGPPHC/2017/747.html.

48 Ruling in the matter of *President of the Republic of South Africa v Office of the Public Protector and Others (Economic Freedom Fighters and Others intervening)*, North Gauteng High Court, Pretoria, 13 December 2017, www.saflii.org/za/cases/ZAGPPHC/2017/748.html.

49 Ibid.

50 Makhele, 'How is Ace Magashule not fit to be ANC SG', News24, 17 June 2017, www.news24.com/news24/MyNews24/how-is-ace-magashule-not-fit-to-be-anc-sg-20170617.

51 Tammy Peterson, 'ANC says commission of inquiry is the only recourse in state capture saga', News24, 13 December 2017, www.news24.com/news24/SouthAfrica/News/anc-says-commission-of-inquiry-is-the-only-recourse-in-state-capture-saga-20171213.

CHAPTER 12

52 Yolandi Groenewald, 'Naspers won't renew contract with Gupta-linked ANN7', News24, 31 January 2018, www.news24.com/fin24/tech/companies/naspers-wont-renew-contract-with-gupta-linked-ann7-20180131.

53 Ibid.

54 Sibongakonke Shoba, 'Hawks go after Themba Maseko', TimesLive, 22 July 2018, www.timeslive.co.za/news/2018-07-21-hawks-go-after-themba-maseko/.

55 A transcript of my testimony before the Zondo Commission, together with supporting affidavits, is available on the commission's website; see www.statecapture.org.za/site/hearings/date/2018/8/30.

56 Dario Milo (for Webber Wentzel attorneys), 'Response to submissions made by former President Jacob Zuma', 19 July 2019, twitter.com/Eusebius/status/1153310209252765696/photo/1.

57 Staff reporter, 'NPA's Cronje delighted with amendments to State Capture commission's regulations', EWN, 29 July 2020, ewn.co.za/2020/07/29/npa-s-cronje-delighted-with-amendments-to-state-capture-commission-s-regulations.

POSTSCRIPT

58 News24Wire, 'How Nkandla's R3.9 million "fire pool" works', BusinessTech, 28 May 2015, businesstech.co.za/news/government/88896/how-nkandlas-r3-9-million-fire-pool-works/.

59 Amanda Khoza, 'Dlamini's "smallanyana skeletons" coming to haunt her – DA', News24, 10 March 2017 www.news24.com/news24/SouthAfrica/News/dlaminis-smallanyana-skeletons-coming-to-haunt-her-da-20170310.

60 The term 'politically exposed person' is not used here in the same sense as in international financial regulation, where it refers to someone who has been entrusted with a prominent public function and generally presents a higher risk for potential involvement in bribery and corruption by virtue of their position and the influence they may hold. In South Africa, the Financial Intelligence Centre has amended the Financial Intelligence Centre Act 38 of 2001 to refer to such an individual as a politically influential person instead of a politically exposed person. See en.wikipedia.org/wiki/Politically_exposed_person#South_Africa.

61 Mandy Wiener, *The Whistleblowers* (Johannesburg: Pan Macmillan, 2020).

Index